LUCKY 13

Edited by Red Shuttleworth

Lucky 13

SHORT

PLAYS

ABOUT

ARIZONA,

NEVADA,

AND

UTAH

University of
Nevada Press
Reno Las Vegas
London

Western Literature Series
Editor: John H. Irsfeld
*A list of books in the series
appears at the end of this
volume.*

The paper used in this
book meets the requirements
of American National Standard
for Information Sciences—
Permanence of Paper for Printed
Library Materials, ANSI Z39.48-1984.
Binding materials were selected for
strength and durability.

University of Nevada Press
Reno, Nevada 89557 USA
New material copyright © 1995 by
University of Nevada Press
All rights reserved
Book design by Richard Hendel
Printed in the United States
of America

9 8 7 6 5 4 3 2 1

Library of Congress
Cataloging-in-Publication Data
Lucky 13 : short plays about Arizona,
Nevada, and Utah / edited by Red
Shuttleworth.
p. cm. — (Western literature series)
ISBN 0-87417-263-2 (acid-free paper)
1. American drama—West (U.S.)
2. Arizona—Drama. 3. Nevada—Drama.
4. Utah—Drama. I. Shuttleworth, Paul,
1944– . II. Title: Lucky thirteen.
III. Series.
PS561.L83   1995
812'.54083279—dc20   94-48932
CIP

FOR MY CHILDREN

Maura, Ciara, Luke Appling & Jessi

CONTENTS

Theatre people like the night. Usually that's when the work gets done and when, later, one has to find a way to come down from performance highs. It's past three in the morning as I write this for you. I've just been out on the back porch. The local coyotes have been in good voice. Probably they've killed and eaten something to their taste. There's a new-covered four-foot-deep hole out back, only forty or so yards from the porch. My children had a coyote funeral.

This is to be a preface to a collection of plays set in the Southwest, so I'll try to shorten this opening saga. But imagine we're together tonight, maybe after seeing a play in, say, Fallon, Nevada. After some Jim Beam 'n water, I'd tell you about my half-coyote, how my oldest daughter redomesticated this creature, and how I'd promised this aged relic of wildness a tour of her natural, most natural territory.

But my half-coyote was half-blind, half-deaf, and skittish in a car. She still liked to find something dead, hog or calf, to clean up. But by the time she adopted us she was a bit worn out. She was at least a dozen years old and wasn't up for any adventure. Not quite up for the best drive in America, for the drive home.

The theatre people I care most for, the playwrights who count most to me, imagine and reimagine and mirror coyote country. There are more playwrights in America than ever before. As my friend Ethan Phillips recently pointed out at the Sundance Institute Playwrights' Lab, playwrights are as plentiful as deer, and the herd probably ought to be thinned out with high-powered rifles. But not in coyote country. Nevada, Utah, and Arizona are only now enjoying a fair share of writers for theatre. In *Lucky 13* you'll encounter what I think of as the First Wave, the pioneers of a new Theatre of the West.

As I was making notes toward this preface, having just returned after a couple of weeks away trying to make theatre in Utah, my wife told me the half-coyote had gone to sleep under an apple tree about a week ago and had failed to wake up.

The best place to read this anthology is on the road from Jackpot, Nevada, to Beaver, Utah, with a stop in Ely. If, like the dead half-coyote, you can't make that drive, where you are will just have to do. But if you can, rent a ragtop Cadillac, stock it with music that will fit the land (I prefer Willie Nelson's "Who'll Buy My Memories" and the Eagles' "Desperado"). Start by dropping fifty dollars in a Jackpot casino, stop for a night in the Sage Best Western in Wells, make a journal/diary entry in Currie, wander around Ely and speak to strangers about their troubles and desert-rat dreams, stop the car at 9,600 feet on Frisco Peak in Utah and—if no cars are coming—stretch out on your back on the road and stare at passing clouds, then have a burger in the railroad town of Milford, and walk the crumbling town of Beaver. I believe you'll find home in both the plays of this volume and in their locales.

The plays in *Lucky 13* speak not of a continental consensus reality, but to and for and of sensibilities grounded in a specific territory, coyote country. These plays arrive from a national interior of myths so profoundly rooted in the national psyche that we keep returning to these myths repeatedly, as if they retain currency. The promise of limitless growth, the cowboy, resources and riches beyond imagination, wilderness: these notions condition who we are in the West and Southwest.

The plays of *Lucky 13* come from a consciousness formed by the land. The characters are battling limits, refusing the fate of past errors. These characters often seek new beginnings, however flawed or tainted by past choices. The plays of *Lucky 13* explore symptoms, pose questions, and ask that readers and audiences participate in locating answers. And I believe these plays also transcend concerns of place and reflect rather universal concerns about the human condition.

All that said, there is great diversification-in-progress among the playwrights. These are thirteen defined, unique visions of Arizona, Nevada, and Utah. There are also dramaturgical differences in form, style, and structure. Arranged according to author's year of birth, *Lucky 13,* from Jerry L. Crawford to Mark Jensen, displays the variety of thought and vision, the trajectory of dramatic thought in a portion of the West.

In Crawford's *St. Viators,* we see a cause-and-effect world, but Christopher Danowski's *Family Values* transgresses the rules from Aristotle; sometimes there are effects with no apparent causes in a Danowski play. Crawford and Danowski were born more than thirty years apart, and some differences in their lives are borne out in their plays. In Crawford's play, the characters are attempting to salvage and re-create a family with love and compromise. Danowski's people are estranged, but they imagine, toss fantasies of family life at each other, and yearn for the old days of nuclear families. We soon realize that they don't have the money in the bank to move out of paralysis and that they are cruising on hopes and dreams in a barren place.

During the brief time I taught English composition at the University of Nevada, Las Vegas, I asked the students in each class how many of them had been raised on farms and ranches. Usually one or two hands would be raised in a class of twenty-five. Then I would ask how many of my students' parents had grown up on farms or ranches. Soon we learned that far more than half the students had grandparents with rural backgrounds. The first group was vaguely sheepish about admitting they were from cow or crop country. The last group enjoyed a romantic notion of their rural heritage. Clearly we are a nation of the rurally dispossessed. The playwrights in *Lucky 13* give voice to this condition, to the rapid depopulation of the once wide-open West, to the myths and realities of the high 'n lonesome. This is coupled with the enormous and problematic population gains in Las Vegas, Phoenix, and even St. George, Utah. The plays in *Lucky 13* take hard looks at the changes and the new contingencies and expectations. The playwrights put new spins on old myths.

In David Kranes's *Cantrell*, the cool gunslinger is a Mafia-type hit man who wants to retire. He happens upon a young lady in distress. The cowboys aren't quite the good guys. I'm oversimplifying Kranes's *Cantrell*, of course; his protagonist is on a complex journey of discoveries that will redefine his life and place him in a new Western context. Kranes was born in 1937.

In *The Total Meaning of Real Life*, Julie Jensen, born in 1942, twists the Western movie version of the West. Girl is on her way to commit suicide when she chances into a Las Vegas marriage chapel and encounters Creepy Guy. Using the movie gunfighter myth, they learn how to re-create themselves, if with only temporary results.

For John D. Newsom, born in 1953, it's important to return to the pre-movie West, to rip the scab off and really look at social ills as dealt with in 1890 in Prescott, Arizona. Newsom's *Dance Saturday Night* tosses us back into our cowboy past, all right, but the play ricochets us to our present, lingering problems with racism.

In each play, the setting conditions the choices that can or must be made by the characters, and the settings are Western. While Kranes's play is set in a bar and in a motel, and Gus Edwards's *Old West* is set in a bar, and my play, *This Is Dead Level,* is set in a motel, the locales in *Lucky 13* are varied, taking the reader to a nice rental home in Las Vegas, a museum, the Butchko Home for Eating Disorders, a Las Vegas wedding chapel, a remote ranch, and the outside of an old-time dance hall. Bob Mayberry's *The Catechism of Patty Reed* takes us to the days of the Donners on Donner Summit. Danowski's *Family Values* places us on raw desert.

As you read, then, from Crawford to Mark Jensen, the First Wave playwrights of Nevada-Utah-Arizona will share with you the first dramatic visions of this territory. One night in Las Vegas, two-time Pulitzer Prize dramatist Edward Albee told a large University of Nevada, Las Vegas, audience, "The job of the playwright is to hold a mirror up to his audience, to say we are now seeing ourselves clearly, to ask if we want to change." The *Lucky 13* plays challenge us much as Albee demands a play ought to challenge. The reader might perceive a consistency of dark vision from play to play, might say the characters in these plays are "wasted, existential people who have little life and almost no hope." But notice how these characters do struggle, do dream, do aspire to better lives and a generosity of spirit and hope. I believe that this bluntly honest group of plays may well lead to the substantial rethinking and reimagining of Western myths and realities.

Perhaps it all began the day Jerry L. Crawford arrived in Las Vegas to teach theatre at the University of Nevada, Las Vegas, in 1962. It wasn't long before Crawford was nourishing the growth of playwrights while building his own distinguished writing career.

Taking the long historical view, an optimistic one, the writers in this anthology have given us the crest of the First Wave. The plays in *Lucky 13* come from playwrights who have been awarded fellowships, prizes, and who have been produced in New York, Los Angeles, Minneapolis, Detroit, and numerous other cities in both professional and academic theatres.

Soon another wave of playwrights will arrive to build on this work, to enlarge part of the vision, to reject another part. For now, the *Lucky 13* plays represent the achievements gained. Naturally, in editing this collection, I hope its publication leads to numerous productions of the authors' full-length plays and of the short plays at hand.

Those productions may or may not happen in the territory written about in *Lucky 13*. While the playwrights have arrived, the theatres have not.

Regionally, production slots for new plays are scarce.

A few theatres in Arizona present new plays. Actors Theatre of Phoenix supports four new plays a year with minimum budgets in its Brown Bag Theatre. Tucson's Arizona Theatre Company has a reading series for new plays, and Borderlands Theater, also in Tucson, produces new work by playwrights of color. Several new theatre ventures, The Unlikely Theatre Company in Tempe and Planet Earth in Phoenix, devote themselves to new plays.

In Utah play development (not production) is on the upswing. Sundance Playwrights' Lab is again working on new plays after a two-year break. Sundance Children's Theatre produces as well as develops new plays. The Utah Shakespearean Festival began its own plays-in-progress program in 1993, giving four full-length plays developmental workshops and staged readings. The Sundance Playwrights' Lab is high-powered, stiffly competitive for the nine slots each July, and has a history of national impact that includes two recent participants' (Robert Schenkkan and Tony Kushner) winning Pulitzer Prizes for plays developed "on the mountain." The Utah Shakespearean Festival's new-play program is in its infancy, but with the prospect of having a new theatre devoted entirely to the "future Shakespeares" (ones primarily rooted in the West), this program may one day make a significant contribution to a Theatre of the West.

The Salt Lake Acting Company, despite staff turnover, remains deeply committed to contemporary and new plays. They are building an intimate theatre space for "risky works." These new works will be cast with actors who will volunteer their work.

Nevada's theatre picture is unfortunately out of balance. Thanks to the energies of faculty and staff at the University of Nevada, Las Vegas, with their keen vision of a Second Wave of playwrights in the making, the University has produced more than sixty new plays by over forty playwrights since 1988. Not a bad record. Although most of the work was student-generated, it is still an extraordinary achievement.

What is dismaying is that once you leave the University of Nevada, Las Vegas, campus, there are no new plays being done in Nevada. Well . . . not quite true. The Rainbow Company in Las Vegas does produce new works for children. And another theatre group, a very small one, produces adaptations and collages from other genres.

What is wrong is that every single one of the theatres in Nevada that claims professional status avoids new writing for the theatre. The combined budgets of Nevada's (several) professional theatres add up to well over $300,000. Each of these theatres will tell you that it is the *only* professional one, that the others are "community theatres." But if you look at their season offerings over the past decade, you'll see that they all tend to cycle through the same works: museum theatre (*Death of a Salesman*), and Neil Simon's works, and other Broadway bouncers finally arriving in half-flawed productions (I think *I'm Not Rappaport* was done by all the theatres in Las Vegas within a two-year period).

Even if we take into account money spent on adaptations and collages from other genres, only 2 percent of Nevada's entire "professional theatre" budget was tossed into new play production in 1993.

Why? Why this disregard of new plays? One theatre leader in Las Vegas has claimed that the demographics just aren't here to do new plays. These economic disincentives disheartened this individual: A Noel Coward production had outsold by far an old Sam Shepard play. The gloss is new plays have dwindled the audience for theatre. This is a ridiculous theory, of course, since no new plays have been produced outside of the safety and support of the University of Nevada, Las Vegas, in the entire history of Las Vegas (except children's plays). If one builds an audience for what is essentially the theatre of approved community standards, a theatre that asks not a serious moral or philosophic question, and a theatre devoted to the tastes of those who wish for little but mindless entertainment, one can hardly expect that audience to suddenly embrace new plays.

If Nevada's theatre directors like producing the works of dead or British writers (a very difficult distinction to be made here), there's little that contemporary Western playwrights can do to change their minds. But culture doesn't begin for Nevada in London. Nor does it, nor should it, arrive via New York City, a place as alien to most Westerners as downtown Calcutta.

Few theatre people I know in the Southwest (producers) would find their theatre's season "unbalanced" if four of six shows were written by Brooklyn playwrights (Arthur Miller, Woody Allen, Israel Horovitz, and Neil Simon). But one theatre a few years back dropped a Sam Shepard play after it signed on a play of mine. The producer explained, "You can't have Shepard and Shuttleworth on the same season." Madness. On top of this madness is the obvious shame and loathing these producers feel for the place where they and their patrons live. Often, I think, especially in Nevada, the producers avoid indigenous playwrights out of a fear of acknowledging the validity of our experience of the West in general and of Nevada in particular. New Yorkers are apparently never "provincial," but those writing in the West are?

The picture in Nevada is not entirely bleak. The Nevada State Council on the Arts (NSCA) stands ready to support (and has a history of supporting) the creation and production of new plays. The NSCA funded a pair of new one-act plays recently done at the Churchill Arts Council in Fallon (coproduced, predictably, by the University of Nevada, Las Vegas). The NSCA has also recently awarded fellowships to three playwrights.

At issue is this anthologist's hope that the plays and playwrights of *Lucky 13* will, indeed, be produced in the region they were inspired by, located in, and devoted to.

When playwright Julie Jensen recently gave an instructive lecture at the University of Nevada, Las Vegas, she hit on at least a chunk of the problem:

> In spite of a regional theatre movement which saw the creation of several hundred professional theatres in the last twenty years, playwrights still have no full-time employment. Disgusting, horrifying, deplorable. Especially when you consider the kinds of people who are hired: accountants, box-office personnel, development people, PR folks, dramaturges, artistic directors, associate artistic directors, assistant artistic directors, designers, technicians, and actors. And not a single playwright. Something is horribly amiss.

She goes on to suggest that every professional American theatre hire one playwright to just be a playwright, to just write plays for his or her theatre. This would provide "two hundred jobs for playwrights," Jensen estimates. "It sounds like a dream come true, doesn't it? And that speaks to the extent of our deprivation." She went on to say that a room filled with artistic directors would squirm about and have gastric disturbances at the very notion. "Fear and loathing for playwrights" is at the core of the problem.

Perhaps we'll never see Jensen's dream come true.

But playwrights may soon lobby arts councils to rewrite grant application requirements for theatres. Perhaps it is time to require publicly funded theatres to do new plays—actual productions, not just readings, which are an excuse to do nothing.

I believe the playwrights in this collection want nothing more than the best drive in America, the drive home: productions in the territory they write from. They want their work performed in coyote country.

So what will make theatres change, make them want to take on new plays? Why can't Jon Jory's Actors' Theatre of Louisville (ATL) be the model? From the very genesis of ATL, Jory said his theatre could only build a reputation by doing new work, not by doing more Shaw, Brecht, and Coward. Jory and ATL have moved American theatre. The paradigm is obvious.

Regional theatres and those in imitation have ossified.

As Julie Jensen hopes, the new will bubble up. The various M.F.A. programs in theatre are pouring out actors, directors, and play-wrights. These new theatre artists are rapidly realizing that they are essentially locked out. A storefront theatre revolution is under way in San Francisco, Phoenix, Tempe, Seattle, and it will reach Reno and Las Vegas.

And theatre artists may well return to hometowns like Fallon, Elko, Ely, and Tonopah. Imagine, for instance, a new play circuit, with theatres in six different Nevada cities and towns cycling new plays throughout the state. By my reckoning, it will happen in the not-too-distant future. At that time, certain theatres, theatres now avoiding new plays, will want to change. And playwrights will welcome that change.

As you read the plays in *Lucky 13*, please enjoy the knowledge that you are among the first to become acquainted with the First Wave. I trust that the very reading of these plays will hasten the day when you'll be able to see these and other new plays in a theatre near you.

Red Shuttleworth

JERRY L. CRAWFORD

Facelifting at St. Viators

Jerry L. Crawford (1934–) recently retired after thirty-two years at the University of Nevada, Las Vegas, where he served as a professor of theatre arts, dramaturge, Barrick Distinguished Scholar, playwright-in-residence, and founding head of the M.F.A. playwriting program. There have been over a dozen professional productions of his plays, including performances at Circle Repertory Company, The Actors Studio, and the Hartman Theatre. In 1991 he received a Nevada State Council on the Arts Playwriting Fellowship. His latest plays are *The Brother's Silence* (about Robert F. Kennedy's final days) and *Eniwetok* (an investigation of a tragedy in the South Pacific during World War II). He is currently working on two baseball screenplays. Crawford travels frequently with the Cleveland Indians as a sports journalist and freelance writer. He is also a literary seminar director for the Utah Shakespearean Festival.

To my children,

Mitch, Vali, and Keli

Charlie Grover

an earnest young boy, nine years of age (Note: If casting is a problem, this age can be "stretched" to ten, eleven, or twelve, or to an actor able to present a nine- to twelve-year-old boy convincingly.)

Debbie Grover

Charlie's mother, a practical, attractive, hardworking housewife; age thirty-five

Mike Grover

Charlie's father, an energetic, athletic, good-looking man; a "blackjack" dealer; age thirty-seven

Father O'Clary

a short, heavy, balding, and garrulous Catholic priest; he admits to being "over age sixty"

TIME

The present, spring

PLACE

The kitchen of a low-budget but nice rental home in Las Vegas, Nevada

SET

A round table with three kitchen chairs; a small sink, counter, and cupboard unit; a small stove and refrigerator. A door at right to a hall; a door and a window at left to the small backyard, which is partially visible far down left and represented by an old tree stump with a very crude makeshift "treehouse" ("stumphouse"?) on its flat top. The "treehouse" is little more than a piece of three-quarter-inch plywood with a couple of walls, one upstage and one left (hence it is open right and front). A tiny window is in the left wall. The back or upstage wall has colorful printing on it: "Charlie's Rooste." A blanket covers the floor. There is one strange object in the corner: a little blue doll cradle with a girl's baby doll and blanket in it. The name "Ella Sue" has been printed neatly on the downstage end of the cradle.

The kitchen set must be upstage sufficiently to permit a key scenic unit to either "fly" in directly in front of it or be slid or moved into that position. This unit should be strategically placed to cut off the furniture, sink, and counter units, and so on, from view yet leave a distance of at least ten to fifteen feet from the "key scenic unit," or at least that much distance between it and any member of the audience. (The alternate solution might be to fly or move this key scenic unit into place *upstage* of the kitchen set, but this would require shifting the kitchen area out of view— there is a space of time that could be used for this shift by lowering lights and indicating a passing of time and a change of locale. However, in the interest of maintaining continuity and a "single set" concept, it may be best to use the former solution and simply place the kitchen upstage far enough to get this new unit in front of it.) The "key or new scenic unit" is just a wall or a flat/drop with a *firm backing surface* that represents the front or the facade of St. Viators Guardian Angel Shrine/Church. This "wall" should be painted as a mosaic in the colors and manner sketched below. When Charlie "attacks" the wall with his "baggie-bombs," a washable solution should be used that will not permanently mar the painting. Thus the wall can be easily cleaned after each performance. Those who "enter" this shrine/church need merely walk around one end toward unseen doors at the side of the "building." Note that the building is triangular, a prism shape; a rectangular lower section supports the triangular overstructure.

(The lights rise on the kitchen. It is an early sunny Sunday morning. Birds are heard in the yard and beyond. The hall door opens and CHARLIE *enters. He wears jeans, a short-sleeve plaid shirt, and Nike canvas shoes. He sleepily fixes himself a bowl of Wheaties and exits into the yard. He climbs into his Roost and sits against the upstage wall of it, eating and gazing out front, up, and around, squinting at the sunlight. His eyes finally rest on the cradle beside him. He rocks it a bit. Then he looks up into the sky and speaks between spoonfuls of Wheaties. As he talks, his conversation alternates between the sky and the cradle with its doll.)*

CHARLIE *(to the sky)*: 'Mornin', Ella Sue.
　　(Pause; chews.)
'Nother *nice* day in paradise, as Mom would say.
　　(Chews.)
Dad would say, " 'Nother *shitty* day in paradise."
　　(He grins and shakes his head.)
Well, it sure is a nice day today, Ella Sue, but yesterday was terrible. Jus' terrible.
　　(Chews.)
I got in big trouble. Big, big trouble.
　　(He rocks the cradle.)
I wonder if sometimes God in heaven lets you come down at night an' play with your ole doll? I wonder. Father O'Clary says He is a kind an' merciful God. After all, you were jus' barely school-age when He took you away.
　　(Chews.)
Danged ole pee-monia.
　　(He looks up at the sky, squinting.)
See, I keep your doll an' cradle up here, jus' in case. An' like I promised you at that hospital, I talk to you ev-ry chance I get. An' I always will, Ella Sue.
　　(The last spoonful of Wheaties.)
Wheaties—breakfast of champions. Dad says I gotta eat lots of Wheaties an' grow past six feet tall if I'm gonna play basketball for Mr. Tarkanian an' his Runnin' Rebels! Tark the Shark.
　　(Pause.)
Boy, I sure got a long ways to go for six feet.
　　(Pause.)
Well, the big, big trouble. It all started Sunday. The day after my

birthday. It sure was a nice birthday, Ella Sue. Our cousin Albert, you remember him? He came up on a bus from Barstow. Only a year to go an' I'll be ten. I can't hardly wait.

(*The lights begin a cross-fade to a flashback.*)

So, Sunday morning Mom got me up at seven bells, as Dad says, to go to eight o'clock mornin' Mass. At St. Viators Guardian Angel Shrine. Over by the Strip. I guess Las Vegas has more bright lights than any other place in the world. Mom says what most people don't know is that Las Vegas has more churches than any other place in the world, too. Wonder why that is? Anyhow, maybe you remember, Mom likes to go to *morning* Mass. That keeps the rest of Sunday free. Ain't so crowded early in the morning either.

(DEBBIE GROVER *enters, tying an apron over her plain print dress. She still wears house slippers, but her hair is up, and her light makeup is on. She begins to prepare a breakfast of eggs, bacon, and toast. She heats water for instant coffee. As she does this,* CHARLIE *climbs down from the Roost and enters the kitchen.*)

DEBBIE: Good morning, Charlie . . .

CHARLIE: Mornin', Mom.

(*He gets himself a glass of milk and sits at the table.*)

DEBBIE: Set the table for you and your father.

CHARLIE: Yes, ma'am.

(*He begins the task.*)

Ain't you gonna eat, too?

DEBBIE: "Aren't," not "ain't." Just coffee and toast for me . . .

CHARLIE: Saucer with your cup?

(*She smiles and shakes her head no.* MIKE GROVER *enters. He wears old jeans, a Rebels sweatshirt, and Nike canvas shoes.*)

'Mornin', Dad.

(MIKE *smiles and ruffles* CHARLIE'*s hair as he goes to the hot water; he makes himself a cup of coffee.*)

MIKE: Nice day . . .

DEBBIE (*unhappily*): Right out of winter into summer. Oh, for a nice, long midwestern *spring*.

MIKE: I'll take the desert anytime.

DEBBIE: Well, you're a native.

CHARLIE: Me, too, huh?

MIKE: That's right, bub, you an' me an' Ella Sue, all native Vegans!

(*He looks up at* DEBBIE, *realizing what he has said; she has given no reaction, but she works at the stove.*)

Debbie there's a native Kansan! Poor thing.

CHARLIE: Will I ever get to see Kansas?

DEBBIE: Someday we'll make a trip back to Lawrence. I still have an uncle there.

MIKE (*looking at his watch*): Hey! Looka the time! Get the ball, bub, we gotta hurry. Never mind breakfast, Deb. He an' I'll eat after the game.

DEBBIE (*firmly*): Hold it.

(*Pause.*)

Just hold it. I'm not going through this again, Mike. It's Sunday.

MIKE: I know what day it is.

DEBBIE: How can you do this every week?

MIKE (*sets his cup down firmly*): I could say the same thing.

DEBBIE (*intensity rising*): Charlie and I go to Mass every Sunday morning.

MIKE (*just as intensely*): Charlie and I play basketball every Sunday morning.

DEBBIE: Play *after* Mass!

MIKE: I told you last week. Some of the guys can't make it later. We gotta play at eight.

DEBBIE: Mass is at eight.

MIKE: Go to a later Mass!

DEBBIE: It's too crowded! I have other things to do. We go at eight. Move your game back.

MIKE: I told you. Some of the guys have jobs, Deb. We play at eight!

DEBBIE: Then you play without Charlie!

MIKE: No! He plays!

DEBBIE: Basketball does not keep a good Catholic from Mass!

MIKE: *I* am not Catholic!

DEBBIE: Well, Charlie is! You agreed when we got married! I'm holding you to it, Mike. Charlie goes to Mass.

(*They are beginning to shout.*)

MIKE: I'm sick of it! *This* Sunday he plays basketball!

DEBBIE: You agreed! You promised!

MIKE: Next thing you'll want *me* to go!

DEBBIE: It wouldn't hurt you! When was the last time you were in *any* church!

MIKE: Ella Sue's funeral!

> (*Dead silence; a long pause;* DEBBIE's *head goes down; tears. She turns to the stove. He touches her gently.*)

I'm sorry.

> (*Pause.*)

Debbie, look, be reasonable. Why is it Charlie's always got Mass or choir every time I want him to do something?

DEBBIE (*recovering; angry; turning with the eggs to the table*): Can I help it your hours are so crazy?

MIKE: I make damn good money! An' I make it honest. How many dealers you know can say the same? I don't gamble, an' I don't run anything on the side! How many can say the same?

> (*Pause.*)

DEBBIE (*quietly*): Not many.

CHARLIE: Can I say somethin'?

MIKE (*ignoring him—following* DEBBIE): It's all bullshit anyway! Mass! Mumbo jumbo!

DEBBIE (*whirling on him*): Don't you speak like that in front of Charlie! Keep that kind of talk out of this house!

MIKE: You knew how I felt when you married me, Debbie.

DEBBIE: I happened to love you just the same.

MIKE: I loved you, too. I married you in your church, don't forget that!

DEBBIE: You said it wouldn't matter with children. They could be raised in the church. You said it wouldn't get in the way of anything!

MIKE: Maybe I was wrong!

DEBBIE: You promised!

MIKE: All right! I promised! But once, just once, couldn't the boy do something for me? It's always you!

DEBBIE: That's not fair! When are you around?

CHARLIE: I think I'll go out to my Roost. . . .

MIKE: You stay here!

DEBBIE: Charlie, get ready for Mass!

> (CHARLIE *stands there confused.*)

MIKE: Sure, take him off to that freak house!

DEBBIE: Freak house? Take that back!

MIKE: That's what it is! Move it fifty yards west, it could be a hell of a casino. Right next to Circus Circus!

DEBBIE (*furious*): St. Viators is the best shrine in town!

MIKE: St. Viators is the ugliest church in America! It's a freak house! The front of that church looks like a nut got loose with a paintbrush and a bottle of scotch!

DEBBIE: That happens to be a beautiful mural! Father O'Clary commissioned it himself!

MIKE: *He* would! He's another joke!

DEBBIE: That man married us!

MIKE: Look, you gotta go to Mass, go to St. Anne's. It's ugly, too, but nothin' like St. Viators!

DEBBIE: St. Viators is my church! It was my mother's church! It was Ella Sue's church! It's Charlie's church!

MIKE: It's a disgrace! It looks like a cheap cartoon!

DEBBIE (*with great anguish*): I reach Ella Sue there!
   (*A long pause.*)

MIKE (*quietly*): I'll play basketball without Charlie.
   (*He exits.*)
   (DEBBIE *sits and cries.* CHARLIE *gets her another cup of coffee. She takes it, then hugs him.*)

DEBBIE: I'm sorry, baby, I'm sorry . . .
   (*She blows her nose; a long pause.*)

CHARLIE: Mom, does Dad believe in God?

DEBBIE: You've asked that before.

CHARLIE: Nobody ever gives me an answer.

DEBBIE: Ask him again.
   (*She reaches for her cigarettes.*)

CHARLIE: Mom, what did he mean when he said I don't ever do things for him?

DEBBIE: He was angry at me. Forget it.

CHARLIE: But what did he mean?

DEBBIE: Since we lost Ella Sue, he thinks you and I are . . . I don't know, too close . . . together too much.

CHARLIE: But I love you both.

DEBBIE: He knows that.

CHARLIE: Does he?
   (*She lights a cigarette.*)
   I wish you'd stop smokin', Mom.

DEBBIE: One of these days, Charlie, one of these days.

CHARLIE: Mom, what does Dad want me to do for him?

DEBBIE: Play basketball, I guess . . .

CHARLIE: But I do once in a while, I do.

DEBBIE: I don't know, Charlie, he's . . .

> (*Pause.*)

We've . . . changed since . . .

> (*She smokes.*)

CHARLIE: Ella Sue.

DEBBIE: She was just a baby. . . .

> (*Long pause; she is choked with grief.*)

CHARLIE: He sure hates St. Viators.

> (*She nods her head.*)

Maybe we should go to St. Anne's today.

DEBBIE (*putting out the cigarette, rising*): St. Viators is our church. That's that.

CHARLIE: It sure makes him unhappy.

> (*She hurriedly clears dishes.*)

It *is* kinda ugly.

DEBBIE: Now don't *you* start. . . .

> (*She wipes her hands.*)

I'll warm up the Buick.

> (*Glancing at her watch.*)

If we hurry, you can take communion. . . .

> (*The lights change again as* CHARLIE *goes into the yard and up into the Roost. He gives the cradle a rock; he squints up at the sky.*)

CHARLIE: On the way to Mass we saw a woman with purple an' yella hair, no kiddin'. Mom said it was "punk." Made me laugh. She an' a big fat kid crossed in front of us at The Landmark. Weird.

> (*Pause.*)

Well, we were late, so I missed communion. Too bad. Friday at confession I had to tell about that swearin' I'd done last week at my friend Howie Stein.

> (*He tucks the blanket around the doll.*)

A new priest gave Mass. He was awful young an' had a squeaky voice. I got to thinkin' about Dad. I knew Mom wasn't about to go to any church 'cept St. Viators. But Dad called it a freak house. I kept thinkin' about the front of that church. . . .

> (*Lights alter; either the wall unit of the church comes in front of the kitchen or it appears behind the kitchen with the latter moving out, whichever accommodates the theatre and*

production. This change can also be done with a complete blackout and a bridge of music to indicate the passing of time.)

The more I thought about it, the more I knew Dad was right! So I made up my mind. I was gonna fix up St. Viators. Well, I figgered I needed some help. All I could think of was Howie, an' I was mad at him. Then I thought of you, Ella Sue! You'd help me. So I took your little Ella Sue doll along with me!

(He picks up the doll and descends. From here on he addresses the doll as though it were his sister, Ella Sue. He strolls around stage looking at the front of the church. He goes close to it; he retreats. He paces. He finally puts the doll down stage left, propped up in a seated position as though looking at the church.)

See? "Prayer. Penance. Peace." You wonder what that means, right, Ella Sue? Well, Father O'Clary says that prayer and penance lead to peace.

(Pause.)

That must be it.

(Pause.)

Boy, the colors are *awful. TERRIBLE.* An' the Christ has that funny thing over His head.

(Looks at doll.)

Halo?

(Pause.)

More like a magic eye. A evil eye! Scares me.

(He goes to sit on the ground, facing the doll.)

Ella Sue, Dad don't love me anymore. No, no, I'm sure. I'm sure.

(Pause.)

He says I never do things for him. He says I'd rather be at that ugly church with Mom than play basketball with him.

(Takes out bubble gum.)

Want some Dubble-Bubble?

(Pause.)

Well, I do.

(He chomps on it.)

Ella Sue, did Dad ever go to church with you?

(Pause.)

I can't remember.

(Pause.)

My buddy Howie Stein goes to Temple Beth Sholom ev-ry

Friday night. That would solve everything for me. If Mass was only on Friday night.

(*To the doll.*)

Y'know, they got a five-thirty afternoon Mass on Saturday. They call it "Mass to Fulfill the Sabbath Obligation." But Mom says it ain't the same.

(*Pause.*)

Aren't the same.

(*Frowns; shrugs.*)

So, it's Sunday, eight bells.

(*He rises and paces silently. Suddenly he whirls and rushes to the doll.*)

Bells! Bells, bells, bong, bang, BOMBS! I got it! Ella Sue, I got it!

(*He picks up the doll and sort of dances with it — explaining to it, pointing to the church, hugging the doll.*)

Bombs! Look, if I fix up St. Viators so it ain't so ugly, Dad won't hate it so bad. An' if I do it just for him, he'll know I love him, an' then he'll love me again!

(*He kisses the doll impulsively — then frowns and sticks out his tongue.*)

Yuk.

(*As lights change, he hurries out and then reappears in a few seconds at his Roost. He climbs into it and puts the doll into the cradle. He takes out a notebook and pencil.*)

OK, let's see now. We gotta have paint. That's easy. A can of white sittin' in the carport. There's a can of red an' a can of yella in the storeroom — left over from paintin' your swing set.

(*Pause.*)

There's a new box of big plastic baggies in the pantry.

(*He writes.*)

I got hundreds of rubber bands. On my paper route ev-ry night I wrap a red rubber band 'round ev-ry *Review-Journal*.

(*Pause.*)

Now, I jus' gotta figure *when* to do it.

(*Pause.*)

Dawn! Like that movie on Channel Five, *Commandos Strike at Dawn!*

(*Happily stretching out; sleepily.*)

I'll jus' get Mom to let me sleep out here like I do lots in warm weather. Then you an' me, Ella Sue, we'll bring Prayer, Penance, and Peace into this family again. You betcha! We'll strike at dawn, Ella Sue, we'll strike at dawn.

(*The stage is going dark.*)

Oh, look, Ella Sue, look. A fallin' star. Make a wish, Ella Sue, make a wish.

(*Pause.*)

Don't tell me now.

(*He yawns happily.*)

I bet we made the same wish . . . jus' like we used to do.

(*The stage goes dark for several seconds; then a slight glow of sunrise appears. A distant bell tolls four.* CHARLIE *stirs. He rouses himself, takes the doll, descends and disappears for a moment. He reappears carrying a cardboard box with his "commando" supplies. "Ella Sue" sits on top of the box. They disappear as lights cross-fade, revealing again the church facade.* CHARLIE *enters. He props the doll up to "observe." He proceeds to make his "baggie-bombs," pouring paint into plastic bags and tying them off with rubber bands as he talks. Several "bombs" should be premade and in the box.*)

I sure miss that Disneyland on TV. 'Specially the cartoon shows. That Roadrunner.

(*He laughs.*)

I feel like that yella-eyed coyote. Gonna get me a roadrunner.

(*Pause.*)

That ain't Disney, is it?

(*Shrugs; proceeds happily.*)

Oh, well. Beats all that crazy Star Wars stuff. Gimme animals ev-ry time.

(*Pause.*)

Hey! We'll mix colors!

(*He pours white, red, and yellow "paint" into one bag and holds it to the light.*)

Bee-utiful!

(*Looks around.*)

Quiet . . . like on that western front.

(*Pause.*)

Ain't nobody around yet.

(*Frowns.*)

Wait a minute. I forgot about *in*side. I better check.

(*He places the baggies on a "firing-line row" and speaks to the doll.*)

You keep an eye out here! I'll be right back!

(*He disappears stealthily around the wall. For several seconds the strange scene holds: a series of colorful baggie-bombs lined up under the watchful gaze of silent "Ella Sue." After a bit,* CHARLIE *dashes back.*)

Shhhhh!

(*Pause; he whispers.*)

Well, I noticed the holy water was awful low. I barely got my fingers wet. I stayed on one knee a second an' looked around. I went up the aisle. Nobody there. Then I looked back up at the balcony. A real pretty, dark-haired lady was sittin' there all alone. With a white veil on her head. It scared the life outta me. I jus' froze. I thought I'd wet my pants for sure. Then she got up an' came downstairs. She walked right past me and smiled. She smelled like vanilla. Boy, was she pretty. The dangdest thing, though. She was smilin', but she was cryin'.

(*Pause.*)

She had a dark green dress on with a metal belt. I thought maybe she was Irish—is this St. Patrick's Day? Bet she was afraid she'd get pinched a lot. The lady went out the side door, through the little chapel on the south.

(*Pause.*)

Anyway, I checked again, Ella Sue. That was it. It was so quiet. All of a sudden, I thought of Dad. An' Mom. An' . . . you. So peaceful. It's sure enough ugly out here, but inside it ain't. All sorts of pretty windows with light siftin' through 'em. Made me feel awful good.

(*He picks up a baggie—a multicolored one.*)

Well, this is it, Ella Sue. Commandos strike at dawn!

(*He winds up.*)

Bombs away for Dad!

(*He hits the wall with a SPLAT. "Paint" spreads and drips in a color spurt.*)

Wow.

(*Another baggie: SPLAT.*)

Wow!

(*Pause; he studies the growing damage.*)

Y'know, Ella Sue, that Christ is a bad drawing. It don't look nothin' like the Christ in books. Makes me mad!

(*Another baggie:* SPLAT! *His anger genuinely comes as he tosses baggie after baggie.*)

That's for Dad an' missin' basketball!

(SPLAT.)

That's for eight o'clock Mass!

(SPLAT.)

That's for catechism!

(SPLAT.)

That's for confession!

(SPLAT.)

That's for communion!

(SPLAT. *He pants; pauses.*)

An' Father O'Clary! "Don't do that! Don't do this!"

(*He winds up.*)

That's for Father O'Clary!

(SPLAT.)

Look, Ella Sue! It's like the fireworks at Disneyland! It's . . . it's Bee-utiful!

(SPLAT. *He laughs*—SPLAT. *He laughs wildly, a fit of joy!* SPLAT. *At the peak of his laughter,* FATHER O'CLARY *enters from down right. He stops short, aghast. He is in a suit, carrying his robe. His neck turns red above his white collar. He is shocked speechless.* CHARLIE *finally senses his presence and turns. He stops laughing. Pause.*)

Hi, Father O'Clary.

(*Pause; silence.*)

Ain't that somethin'? Ain't it?

(*Beat.*)

Aren't it?

(*Silence.*)

Well, d'ya like it? Only took a few minutes.

(*Silence.*)

Free of charge.

(*Silence.*)

I sure wish Dad was here.

(*Suddenly* FATHER O'CLARY *goes into action. He grabs* CHARLIE *roughly by the back of his shirt collar.*)

FATHER O'CLARY: Charlie Grover! Have you gone crazy?

CHARLIE: What?

FATHER O'CLARY: Charlie, Charlie, God in Heaven, you've gone crazy!

CHARLIE: Oh, no, sir, I think it's Bee-utiful! Dad'll love it!

FATHER O'CLARY: Your father and mother . . .

> (*He chokes off in a rage.*)

Sit down! Sit, I say!

> (CHARLIE *sits, trembling, next to the doll.*)

Don't you move! Do you understand me? Do you?

CHARLIE: Yes, sir. I won't, I won't!

FATHER O'CLARY: Sit right there while I call your parents! I'll be right back!

> (*He heads off to the church.*)

Don't you move! Not one inch!

> (*He is gone;* CHARLIE *turns glumly away from the doll and looks skyward out center; lights change again; the upstage area and the church go dark.*)

CHARLIE: Ever seen a priest mad, Ella Sue?

> (*Pause.*)

I thought my dad had a temper. Nothin' like Father O'Clary. He came back after the phone call an' had another fit. No kiddin'. He got Mr. Swanson, the janitor. It was terrible. Mr. Swanson laughed at first! Boy, that made Father O'Clary even madder! I thought he'd pop his collar. He kept askin' me why I did it, but ev-ry time I opened my mouth to explain, he'd yell at me to be quiet.

> (*Pause.*)

Then Mom an' Dad got there. I was scared half to death by that time. Wow, you'd think I'd killed somebody. I felt like a crim-nal for sure. Mom started cryin'. Of course. I heard Father O'Clary say somethin' about "thousands of dollars."

> (*Pause.*)

Then Father O'Clary took Mom inside. She was sobbin' her eyes out. I felt sick. Sick as all get-out. I was ready to chuck up my guts when Dad came out of the church an' walked toward me. . . .

> (*Lights change and rise again;* MIKE *enters from around the church and walks toward* CHARLIE.)

I figgered this was it for sure.

(*Pause.* MIKE *stares at* CHARLIE, *then at the wall.* MIKE *walks slowly down right and lights a cigarette.*)

MIKE: Charlie.

CHARLIE: Yes, sir.

MIKE: Come here, son.

CHARLIE: Yes, sir.

(*He walks to* MIKE.)

MIKE: Now tell me, Charlie, why did you do it?

(*Long silence;* CHARLIE *cannot find the words. Finally, the dam breaks, and* CHARLIE *begins to cry. For a moment* MIKE *just lets him cry. Then the crying turns to sobs, and* MIKE *kneels to take the boy into his arms. The tears subside.*)

That's better. Gotta be a man now.

(*He gives the boy a handkerchief.*)

Charlie, now tell me. Why did you do it?

CHARLIE: I . . . I thought you'd like it.

MIKE: What?

CHARLIE: I did it . . . for you.

(*Long pause.*)

MIKE: What do you mean?

CHARLIE: You said it was ugly.

MIKE: Charlie . . .

CHARLIE: You called it a freak house.

MIKE: Charlie, I didn't mean . . .

(*He sighs, breaks off.*)

Charlie, I spoke in anger. I . . .

CHARLIE: You said I never do things for you, but see, I do!

MIKE (*sitting*): Oh my God . . .

(CHARLIE *sits by him.*)

Charlie, I didn't mean . . . well, I didn't mean it just the way I said it.

CHARLIE: But it's what you said.

(*Pause.* MIKE *drags on the cigarette.*)

I sure wish you an' Mom would quit smokin', Dad.

(MIKE *puts out the cigarette.*)

MIKE: Charlie, do you know what the cost of the damages is here? Do you have any idea?

CHARLIE: Damages?

MIKE: Yes, Charlie, damages. You didn't redecorate, boy, you demolished. All that paint has to be removed. If that's possible.

You just ruined a five-thousand-dollar mosaic mural, boy! Where do you think I can get that kind of money?

CHARLIE: Please don't get mad again, Dad, please. . . .

(*Silence.* MIKE *rubs his eyes.*)

MIKE: Charlie, you just don't understand.

CHARLIE: Yes, sir, I understand. It's going to cost you a lot of money.

MIKE: Charlie, you misunderstood what I said yesterday. I didn't want you to go out and do some damn fool thing like this. To your own church. Your mother's church! Five thousand bucks!

(*He slams his fist into his hand and rises.* CHARLIE *starts to cry again, quietly.*)

CHARLIE: I'm sorry, Dad, I'm sorry. . . .

MIKE: Sorry? A lot of good that does! Five thousand bucks! Christ!

(*He exits into the church.* CHARLIE *sits there, sniffling.* FATHER O'CLARY *and* DEBBIE *enter.* CHARLIE *looks up at them.* FATHER O'CLARY *closes his eyes and sighs a long, long sigh. He then examines the wall. He visibly wilts, turns, and exits to the church again.* DEBBIE *comes to sit by* CHARLIE.)

DEBBIE: Charlie, Charlie, Charlie . . .

(*Silence.*)

Well, you walk on home. Your father and I have to talk some more to Father O'Clary. He said their insurance won't handle something like this.

(*She rises.*)

Oh, Charlie, Charlie, Charlie . . .

(*She exits into the church.* CHARLIE *roams down left as the lights change. He disappears a moment. He reappears and climbs into his Roost with the doll, putting it into its cradle. St. Viators has disappeared; the kitchen is revealed again. However, the light focus is on the Roost.* CHARLIE *squints up at the sky.*)

CHARLIE: Well, Ella Sue, that afternoon I had to go back to St. Viators an' help Mr. Swanson wash down the wall. Didn't help much. I sure did a great job with my baggie-bombs!

(*Pause.*)

Mr. Swanson grinned once an' said, "A reg-lar facelifting."

(*Pause.*)

Father O'Clary an' two other priests came by in a big black car while me an' Mr. Swanson used hoses an' brushes. The three priests turned all red, an' they had to get this one a glass of water an' set him down a spell. The one priest, a very, very old man with snow white hair, well, he said they'd jus' have to "start from scratch." A whole new mural or maybe a whole new wall. Father O'Clary got mad again. He said he'd picked that design an' "by St. Jude it was going to be done the same way again!"

(*Pause.*)

That sure made me awful sad.

(*Pause.*)

Ella Sue, the final showdown was at supper last night.

(*He talks as he descends. Lights change.* DEBBIE *enters and finishes putting food on the table.* MIKE *enters, sits, and eats silently.*)

We had porkchops an' peas an' a green salad with I-talian dressing, my fav-rite. I still love my porkchops, Ella Sue. I like to chew on the bones.

(CHARLIE *sits at the table and chews silently on a porkchop bone.* DEBBIE *sits and eats. Silence for a bit.*)

MIKE: O'Clary called again. He said I could pay the rest off a hundred a month.

DEBBIE: That's very fair of him.

(*Pause.*)

Father O'Clary's a good man.

MIKE: Good man, my foot. I don't even think it's a five-thousand-dollar job. Hell, you can't trust 'em. The righteous priest says right is right an' wrong is wrong. The sinner must pay!

(*Pointing to himself.*)

The innocent must pay! Right in the tradition of the whole goddamn mumbo jumbo.

CHARLIE: Don't cuss, Dad.

MIKE: I hope you noticed the word "mercy" missing on that wall! Five thousand dollars my royal fanny. O'Clary's probly skimmin' off the top for himself. I'm callin' Ted Becker to get over an' take a look at that wall.

DEBBIE: What would Ted know about it? He's a plumber.

MIKE: He'd know. He's no fool. Neither am I. Probly three thousand for the Pope an' a grand for O'Clary. A thousand should easy repair that wall. O'Clary's pullin' a fast one!

DEBBIE: He wouldn't do that. It's mosaic. Very expensive.

MIKE: He's skimmin', I tell you.

DEBBIE: He is not! Mike, he's a priest!

MIKE: So what? He's a priest! This is Vegas! He's skimmin'! Look, he's a dealer just like me—only I don't skim! But we both *deal,* baby, we *deal.* O'Clary an' I deal to people, an' we both have to take them. That's how this town survives.

DEBBIE: Oh, stop it.

MIKE: That's how this country survives!

DEBBIE: I can't take this, Mike, I mean it. Stop it!

MIKE: You can't trust him, Deb! You can't trust anybody! I worked hard for the little we got saved. It took me a year to save—just on tokes. Now I have to throw it and more away! On what? That . . . that mess!

DEBBIE: Mike, there's more than money involved. *We're* responsible!

MIKE: Not me!

DEBBIE: Yes, you! Me! All of us!

MIKE: Sure, blame me!

DEBBIE: If you hadn't said those terrible things about the church, he never would have dreamed of such a crazy fool thing!

MIKE: Did I tell him to go bomb the place with paint?

DEBBIE: You might as well have!

MIKE: Well, fuck it! Just fuck it! I'm not paying five thousand bucks! I'm not payin' a dime! I worked for that money, an' it's not goin' to that goddamn church! Fuck it!

(*She hits him hard. A long, deadly silence.*)

DEBBIE (*quietly, but with deep intensity*): Don't ever say things like that again!

(*Pause; he is furious but holding, holding.*)

And keep your lousy toke money. *I'll* pay for it. I'll go back to work.

MIKE (*exploding*): Go ahead! Be a fool! You an' the kid keep goin' to Mass. Go every day. Say prayers and rattle the beads, do your penance! Fast and light candles! Peace in the valley, Amen! I'm leaving, baby, like I should have done years ago!

DEBBIE: What stopped you? Ella Sue!?!

(*He whirls on her, but doesn't hit her.*)

Take your money and live at the Trop. That's where you'd rather be anyway.

MIKE: You've hit me for the first and last time, baby. You're lucky I didn't deck you.

DEBBIE: That'll be next.

MIKE: I'll be back later for my clothes!

DEBBIE: They'll be in the yard!

MIKE: Fine!

(*He exits. She gets a cup of coffee, lights a cigarette, and sits.*)

CHARLIE: He won't really leave forever, will he?

(*Pause.*)

DEBBIE: No. He'll go over to Vince's bar on Sahara. Eventually, he'll be back. We have tempers, Charlie, it's a fault.

(*Pause.*)

But we love our children. . . .

(*Pause; she gently corrects herself.*)

We love you, Charlie. And we love each other. . . .

(*with great difficulty*)

. . . when all is said and done.

(*Pause.*)

He'll be back.

CHARLIE: Mom, I'm sorry. It's all my fault.

DEBBIE: No, no. It's not all your fault. You did wrong, Charlie, but it's not all your fault.

CHARLIE: Whose fault is it?

DEBBIE: It's how life is, Charlie. It's not so much who's to blame, but who's willing to bear the pain, bear the responsibility, and not even ask who's to blame.

CHARLIE: I don't understand.

DEBBIE: Someday, maybe when you have a child of your own—or, God help you, when they're gone, one way or another, grown up or gone away—then maybe you'll understand.

(*Pause.*)

Have some more milk.

CHARLIE: I'm full.

(*Pause.*)

Mom, why does he always get so mad about spendin' money?

DEBBIE: That's all he really knows, Charlie. His family and his work, his money.

CHARLIE: Did Dad *ever* go to church? Not even when he was a boy?

DEBBIE: No. His family was supposed to be Protestant. Methodist, I think. But they didn't go to church.

CHARLIE: Does goin' to church make all the diff-rence?

DEBBIE (*sighs, flicks ashes*): They say it doesn't, no. Some say that. But me? Well, it's always made the difference for me. It got me through. It's there, I can put my hand on it, my feet. I can put my body there, and the mind follows. There's a bit of . . . peace. Rest.

CHARLIE: But Dad never went to church?

DEBBIE: No, he just goes to work. That's what's there for him.

CHARLIE: Well, is that why he won't love me, 'cause I go to church?

DEBBIE: Don't be silly. He loves you. In his way. He's a dealer, Charlie. He's like a lot of other dealers and people who work in this strange city. They have a kind of . . . passion. For money, baby. Or for pursuing it. Mike grew up in this city. I was luckier. I can't explain it, Charlie. I had Kansas, at least for a while. This is all he's ever seen or known.

(*Pause.*)

He loves you.

CHARLIE: I don't think so, Mom. He knows I believe in God, like you do. I think that's why he won't love us anymore.

(*A long pause; she is searching for words.*)

DEBBIE: No. He just . . . he just wants us to love him . . . as much as we love God.

CHARLIE: Nobody can be loved like God.

DEBBIE: That's right. It's different. Mike just doesn't understand that.

(*Pause.*)

Ella Sue was very special to him, Charlie. And he thinks, well, he thinks . . . if there is a God, God let him down.

(*Pause.*)

That happens to people who have great personal tragedy.

CHARLIE: Do you think God let us down?

DEBBIE: No. He just didn't do us any favors. We have to live with it.

CHARLIE: You're not goin' back to work again, are you? Not back to that dang ole bank?

DEBBIE: I may have to, Charlie. You don't need me here every second anymore. You just grew up more than you realize. Besides, Charlie, we have to do what has to be done.

(*She exits.* CHARLIE *clears the dishes. He leaves for a moment, then returns carrying a basketball. He sits and stares at it. He puts it on the floor and it rolls aimlessly, gently into a corner where it comes to rest. Pause.* MIKE *appears in the yard. He goes to the Roost and peers into it. He gives the cradle a push. It rocks. Silence.* CHARLIE *sees him and goes into the yard. He approaches* MIKE *cautiously. They look at one another for a long moment as the cradle slowly comes to a halt. Before it is totally motionless,* MIKE *reaches in and places a hand on it for the full stop. At that moment, he quietly cries.* CHARLIE *is confused and hurt. He finally just reaches over with one hand and takes his father's free hand.* MIKE *has not let go of the cradle. After a moment, he lets go and they sit down together in silence, still with hands clasped together and their eyes looking up into the sky. Finally,* MIKE *lets go and lights a cigarette.)*

MIKE: My last one, I promise.

(He grins sheepishly at his lie.)

Charlie, I'm gonna make a bargain with your mother. If she's willin' to go to the Saturday afternoon Mass, so we can play basketball at eight bells Sunday, well . . . I'll go to Mass with you.

CHARLIE *(stunned)*: Are you pullin' my ole leg, Dad?

MIKE: No. I mean it.

CHARLIE: Why? What happened?

(MIKE doesn't seem to hear. He is looking at the cradle. He leans over and gives it another little push and watches it rock. Somehow CHARLIE *senses that push was his father's answer. Pause.)*

Dad?

MIKE: Yes, Charlie?

CHARLIE: I'm sorry about what I did.

MIKE: We'll work it out.

(He rises to enter the house. He stops and turns back to look at his son.)

Charlie?

CHARLIE: Yes, sir?

MIKE: Where in the world did you get the idea to do exactly what you did?

CHARLIE: Well, it seemed jus' the right thing to do.

MIKE: Why?

CHARLIE: Well, because I love you as much as I love God. If you didn't like God's house, I thought I'd change it to make you happy. An' you love bright colors an' fireworks, an' you were in the Navy, an' you were sort of a commando an' . . .

(His father laughs and holds up a hand for CHARLIE *to stop.)*

I figgered God wouldn't mind what I did 'cause I figgered God already knew I loved you both, but you didn't.

(Silence.)

MIKE: I love you, Charlie.

(CHARLIE *grins.* MIKE *enters the kitchen, picks up the basketball, and disappears into the house.* CHARLIE *crawls into the Roost, tucks the covers around the doll, and squints up at the sky. Lights change.*)

CHARLIE: Everything's back to normal again, Ella Sue. Sure feels good. Y'know, I heard they were movin' St. Viators across town. The shrine by the Strip's gettin' a new name. That's maybe a good thing. Wonder if we'll follow St. Viators or stay at the building I attacked? Bet we follow St. Viators.

(*Pause.*)

The way I see it, Ella Sue, if you have trouble with your dad, the chances are he really loves you.

(*Puts a piece of Dubble Bubble into his mouth; he chomps.*)

Still, it don't hurt to take things into your own hands sometimes, to be sure.

(*Chews.*)

Just save up on rubber bands an' baggies.

(*He hums as he rocks the cradle with one hand and taps a rhythm on his knee with the other hand. As the lights fade to final darkness, he is squinting up happily and innocently at "Ella Sue."*)

The End

DAVID KRANES

Cantrell

David Kranes (1937–) writes both plays and fiction. He is a graduate of the Yale School of Drama. His plays have been staged at such theatres as the Mark Taper Forum, Long Wharf Theatre, and Manhattan Theater Club. His novels include *The Hunting Years* (1984) and *Keno Runner* (1986). His screenplay *Truants* was produced in 1986. Recent short fiction has appeared in *Esquire*, *Quarterly West*, and the Delacorte Anthology *Dreamers & Desperadoes*. Kranes serves as artistic director of the Sundance Playwrights' Lab and currently directs the graduate creative writing program at the University of Utah.

For Patrick Tovatt

Cantrell was first published in *The Best Short Plays 1988,* edited by Ramon Delgado, Applause, Theatre Book Publishers, 1988.

Cantrell
forty-three, once a hit man

The Hit

The Man

Cowboy #1

Cowboy #2

Utah State Highway Patrolman

Bartender

Chrissie
fifteen, learning

Rupert
thirty-seven, Chrissie's foster father

TIME

Last July

PLACE

We are in — among other places — Las Vegas, a cowboy bar, a motel in Cedar City, Utah.

The back wall of the set is a scribble of neon. Two levels. The upper level upstage, a full U-shaped thrust — the partial arc of a bar and barstools stage right. A café table, chairs, and a jukebox stage left. To the rear of the raised platform is a motel bureau. At the front center of the upper level — situated so that its footboard forms/flows into a car front-seat back on the lower level — is a raked motel bed. The principal areas on the lower level are a golf green stage right and the restraining rail of a canyon overlook stage left. There is a public phone somewhere on the periphery of all this.

Characters move fluidly from space to space within all of this — without interruptive blackouts. Modulations and transitions are covered with current country-and-western music.

(*Lights fade in on the scribble of neon on the back wall. The sound of distant cars moving every once in a while, along Sands Road in Las Vegas.*

A dim pool of light on CANTRELL. *He wears an extremely expensive dark suit and is sitting on the front seat of his car, polishing his gun with a silk ascot. The gun should gleam like an emerald and look murderous. If* CANTRELL *has the radio in his car on, it plays Telemann. Beside* CANTRELL, *on the passenger side of the front seat, sits a portable fridge—plugged into the cigarette lighter.* CANTRELL *interrupts his polishing to open the fridge unit and take out a quality glass and a bottle of expensive Russian vodka. He pours himself a drink, sits sipping it, checking the chamber of the gun.* CANTRELL *will also slip two Ziploc bags over his hands and tighten them.*

We hear a particularly close vehicle. Perhaps some headlights even sweep by CANTRELL. *Whatever the effects—it is what* CANTRELL *has been waiting for. He sets the glass back into the fridge, turns the radio off or lower.*

While CANTRELL *makes his final preparations, we will hear a garage door rolling up and a car moving into the garage.* CANTRELL *is out of his car by the time the garage door begins going down again. In fact, he has moved forward, through the shadows into the "garage space" before we hear the sound of the other car door opening—then closing.*

*There is enough light now to see "*THE HIT.*"* THE HIT *is a man in his forties, also wearing an expensive suit.*)

CANTRELL: This is a historic moment.

THE HIT (*seeing him, startled*): Whoa!

CANTRELL (*advising*): Still. Just . . .

THE HIT (*in his way, he knows*): Wait, wait. Who are . . . ?!

CANTRELL: This is my last.

THE HIT: Don't.

CANTRELL: I'm finished.

THE HIT: I'm serious.

CANTRELL: I do you—and then I don't do this anymore.

THE HIT: Hey, let's talk. Who's paying?

CANTRELL: You can't kill people forever. It's wrong.

THE HIT: Really, we can . . .

CANTRELL: What's the future—you know?

THE HIT: Don't . . .

CANTRELL: Just relax.

THE HIT: Please—really—don't.

CANTRELL: And think of it this way . . .

THE HIT: I'll split town. I'll go away. I won't exist. It'll be the same, you just won't have it on your conscience.

CANTRELL: Think of it this way: no more decisions, no more questions.

THE HIT: Really. Please. Don't. Wait.

> (CANTRELL *will fire three shots. We will see the flares of light from his instrument.*)

CANTRELL: You can change your life.

> (*First shot.*)

A person. Usually I drink the vodka *after* the hit. Do the hit first . . . go back to the car . . . enjoy the vodka. But you can change. You can change the order.

> (*Second shot.*)

I found that! And if you can change the order, then you can change your life. No more killing. No more jobs. It's a wonderful day!

> (*Third shot.*)

Now I get in my car and change my life. I've always wondered what to do with the money (*clip of bills in his hand*) that I get. An amazing thing happened. Today. I was at the MGM Grand . . . by the pool . . . watching what I call the "fish scales," light the sun makes on the pool water—and I started remembering all kinds of tiny pieces of when I was a kid. Time, once, I almost drowned. Now I get in my car and change the order of all the pieces. I drive east. My tank is full. I got my wheels aligned. I've never been east of here. Go to "Utah"!

> (*He laughs; says the word again: he likes its sound.*)

"Utah." Maybe I'll even throw my instrument totally away! It's a wonderful day! It's a historic moment! Cantrell will never again be the same! You can stop doing what you're doing. You can start doing *different* things.

> (*Leaning over the body of* THE HIT.)

Thank you.

> (*Fade the light on the garage. Bring up the Telemann; then modulate it into Willie Nelson. Slow fade up on* CANTRELL, *sitting in front seat of his car, elbow out the window, singing along. Perhaps there's a band of turquoise-blue sky high above.*)

The red/blue turning of a patrol car light behind CANTRELL.
CANTRELL *checks his rearview mirror. He slows. He stops. From
the very rear of the stage, a* HIGHWAY PATROLMAN
approaches—first silhouette, then full. CANTRELL *smiles.*)

PATROLMAN: Good morning.

CANTRELL: Absolutely . . . absolutely. How are you?

PATROLMAN: License and registration, please.

CANTRELL (*searching for license and registration*): That's a wonderful
drive, down through the Virgin River Canyon. The air smells
like fish. One time I went scuba diving. In Lake Mead. And it
was like that. I bought the gear. And I used it once. And it was
wonderful. But I let it go. I never got back. I think what you
need, really, is lifetime activities. Well, now I'm ready for those.
This is the first day of my life. I suppose you've heard that. I may
take up golf.

(CANTRELL *hands his license and registration to the*
PATROLMAN.)

PATROLMAN: I'll be just a moment.

CANTRELL: Take your time.

(*The* PATROLMAN *will walk back about ten paces and stand
with his back to* CANTRELL. CANTRELL *will bellow along with
whatever country-and-western song is on the radio. The*
PATROLMAN *will return to stand beside the "car."*)

CANTRELL: It must be nice—having a uniform. That must be
gratifying. It looks good. It fits well. Maybe someday *I'll* have a
uniform. Who can say?

PATROLMAN: Are you aware, Mr. Cantrell, that you were going
eighty-two miles an hour, twenty-seven miles in excess of the
speed limit?

CANTRELL: I knew it was somewhere around there.

PATROLMAN: I'm going to give you this citation, Mr. Cantrell. You
can mail it. Or I've included an address in St. George.

CANTRELL: "Utah"!

PATROLMAN: Yes, Utah. If you're there after nine this morning, you
can simply go to the courthouse and pay it. It's—I'm sorry—
steep. But you were being very excessive in your speed. You've
got to watch that.

CANTRELL (*handing it out*): Here's one hundred dollars.

PATROLMAN: I'm sorry, Mr. Cantrell. But you've got the wrong
person. I have religious principles.

CANTRELL: I thought you were charging me for speeding.

PATROLMAN: No, sir, the *State* is.

CANTRELL: Oh. The State. Excellent. But don't you work for the State?

PATROLMAN: Yes, sir. But I can't take the State's money.

CANTRELL: Oh. That's fine. I didn't know. Listen . . . Listen, you have a brother?

PATROLMAN: I have *four* brothers, Mr. Cantrell. And three sisters.

CANTRELL (*squinting, appraising*): No. No, up close, I can see. I had a job once. My twenty-third, actually. But . . . no connection, no. I was wrong. Wrong eyes.

PATROLMAN: Mr. Cantrell—sir? Is that a respirator? Beside you? On your front seat and plugged into your dash? I'm sorry. Are you on a respirator? Do you have a medical problem—I'm sorry if I caused any difficulty for you. It just didn't occur to me that . . . ?

CANTRELL (*laughing*): No. No.

PATROLMAN (*backing away*): Good. Well . . . just keep your speed down, then.

CANTRELL: I will . . . I will. You watch. I'm ready.

(*Fade down lights. Fade up music. When the lights and music cross-fade again, we see* CANTRELL *in his motel, at the bureau, on the phone. A piece of expensive luggage sits on the bed.* CANTRELL *still wears his suit.*)

. . . Hello, golf course? This is Cantrell. How are you? Good . . . Cantrell. Listen, I've just checked in here at the Globe Motor Lodge, and I'm ready to take up golf. You open for business? . . . Cantrell. What do I owe you? You have everything I need for this new activity? Do you have everything that I'll have to use? Do you take major credit cards? Or should I bring a cashier's check? Or, if you would prefer, I have some unmarked bills. What does golf cost? If I do it every day for the rest of my life, what's it going to run me?

(*The light begins to fade on* CANTRELL *as he continues on the phone.*)

. . . The Globe Motor Lodge . . . Cantrell . . . I just retired from my former line of endeavor . . . I hit people . . . What does golf cost?

(*The light is down. The music is again up. The music fades down and we hear* CANTRELL's *voice in the dark.*)

This is *great!* This is *it!*

(*Very gradual fade up of light to bright sunlight.*)

This is *great,* man! Fuck hits! Fuck *those* assignments! Fuck *that* life! All right, *golf!* Someone should've told me. This is great!! I love it!

(CANTRELL *is on the course. He has no idea what he is doing, but he is having the time of his life. We have seen him take a swing in the dim light. He has followed the "ball" almost straight above his head with his eyes. By the time the lights are full, a golf ball drops just in front of him, and* CANTRELL *roars with gleeful laughter. He is still in his suit pants, silk shirt with the sleeves rolled up, open vest, wingtip shoes.*)

(*Calling off.*)

Hey . . . ! Hey . . . !

DISTANT VOICE: . . . Yeah . . . ?

CANTRELL (*pointing to himself*): Tom Watson!

(CANTRELL *erupts again with deep, gleeful laughter. Fade the light on* CANTRELL, *having more fun than he has ever had. Light in on the cowboy bar.* CHRISSIE, *a fifteen-year-old trying to be loose and thirty, is near the bar, flirting with two* COWBOYS.)

COWBOY #1: C'mon home with us.

CHRISSIE: You mean—come to your pickup?

COWBOY #2: Home is where you hang yer hat, honey.

COWBOY #1: Haven't you heard that?

CHRISSIE: You guys wanna hang your hats on me—'s that it?

(*The two* COWBOYS *laugh.*)

Gimme some quarters, an' buy me another beer. Nothin's free, ya know.

COWBOY #1: Absolutely!

(*To* COWBOY #2.)

Give Chrissie some quarters.

(*As* COWBOY #2 *does, calling off.*)

Three more draft!

(*By now, the light is also up on the left side of the stage, the table next to the juke where* CANTRELL *sits. He has still not changed— though his hair is slickly brushed. He looks strangely elegant, though very out of place. He is eating a steak.* CANTRELL *has been watching* CHRISSIE *and her scene with the* COWBOYS. *He watches her cross by him to the juke, watches the* COWBOYS

lecherously watching her. CANTRELL *rises and crosses to*
CHRISSIE *at the jukebox.*)

CANTRELL: I want you to come over and sit at my table for a while
with me.

(*He crosses back to his meal.* CHRISSIE *looks at him, a bit
mystified. She makes her last selections with her last quarter,
moves, somewhat defiantly, to the edge of* CANTRELL'S *table.*)

CHRISSIE: So what kind of bullshit was *that*—just then?

CANTRELL: Sit down.

CHRISSIE: Yeah? Who are you?

CANTRELL: Cantrell. Just sit down.

(*Silence.*)

Sit down. I want to talk with you.

(*A beat.* CHRISSIE *sits. The* COWBOYS, *of course, will start
noting this.*)

CHRISSIE: So?

(CANTRELL *nods.*)

So, I'm sitting. So what?

CANTRELL: What are you, sixteen?

CHRISSIE: What are you—my father?

CANTRELL: Fifteen? Seventeen?

CHRISSIE: I'm old *enough.*

CANTRELL: Look . . .

(*The* COWBOYS *are now in conference.*)

You think you're a pro?

(*No answer.*)

You want to be a pro. . . . Fine. Here's two hundred bucks. I'm
buying you for the next hour. You think you're up to that? . . .
Or are you just a mouth?

(CANTRELL *slides the two bills across the table and under*
CHRISSIE'S *hand. She looks at them, unfolds them.* COWBOY #1
has started across the space to CANTRELL'S *table.*)

COWBOY #1: This greaser giving you shit, Chrissie?

CHRISSIE: . . . No.

COWBOY #1: I think he is.

CHRISSIE: Well, he isn't.

COWBOY #1 (*to* CANTRELL): We protect our own, here.

CANTRELL (*picking up his steak knife and fork*): That's admirable.

CHRISSIE (*to* COWBOY #1): Why don't you fuck off, Vern?

COWBOY #1: Don't . . .

CHRISSIE: We're having a conversation.

COWBOY #1 (*to* CANTRELL): This girl's too young. She ain't accountable. She needs close caring for.

CHRISSIE (*standing*): Listen, Vern, I don't need fuck-all! I mean it. So don't . . .

> (CANTRELL *clears his throat and holds his steak knife vertical in a gesture somehow hard not to attend to.*)

CANTRELL (*essentially to* THE COWBOY): I want you to watch. Do I have your attention? I want you to watch.

> (*With one hard-pressed stroke, he cuts the little finger from his left hand.* THE COWBOY *gasps and steps back.* CHRISSIE *shrieks.* CANTRELL *stanches the blood with his linen napkin. He has their attention.*)

You see . . . if I can do that to *myself* . . . I think you've got to think about what I could do to *you*—and to your *friends*.

> (CHRISSIE's *breathing has almost a tiny hum to it in its expiration.* THE COWBOY's *breathing seems to be through mucus.*)

COWBOY #1 (*backing*): . . . Right . . . Right. I get . . . I see.

> (COWBOY #2 *has been edging toward the exit.* COWBOY #1 *joins him—and they are gone.*)

CANTRELL (*to* CHRISSIE): Let's go for a walk.

> (*Fast fade down of light, crossing with music. Fewest necessary beats. Cross-fade in again on the room at the Globe Motor Lodge.* CANTRELL *has the stub of his finger taped and bandaged. He moves while he talks.* CHRISSIE *is on the bed, wide-eyed, watching him.*)

. . . Forty-seven people. Forty-seven assignments. This is not a good line of work. This is not rewarding. There's no pleasure in it. This afternoon, I started playing golf—and it's much better. Tomorrow . . . what's that building in this town? The round one. Just west. At the college. Near the library.

CHRISSIE: It's a "replica."

CANTRELL: "Replica"? What do you mean, "replica"?

CHRISSIE: That's just what it is, asshole. That's just what it's called. "Replica." Don't ask me those questions. "Replica." It's what we learned in school.

CANTRELL: "Replica."

CHRISSIE: It's a big thing here.

CANTRELL: "Replica." . . . "Utah."

CHRISSIE: It's called Shakespeare. Something Shakespeare. It's all famous. They do plays there. Don't ask me about it.

CANTRELL: "Shakespeare" . . . in "Utah" . . . in a "replica."

(CANTRELL *laughs gleefully.*)

I like it. I like it! I like it a lot! . . . So you mean the building's called "Shakespeare"?

CHRISSIE: No. I don't know. They do Shakespeare . . . that's all I know—whatever that is. Jesus Christ, Cantrell! In the summers. Like now. They do Shakespeare's plays.

CANTRELL: . . . Then maybe I'll start doing Shakespeare. Work it in. Around the golf. They do that during the day—do you mean—or at night?

CHRISSIE: I don't know! Night . . . I guess . . . mostly.

CANTRELL: Good . . . here.

(*He extends something to her.*)

CHRISSIE: What?

CANTRELL: Keep this.

CHRISSIE: Your . . . ?

(*She touches her own little finger.*)

CANTRELL: Put it somewhere outside for a couple of weeks. Then keep the bone. Save it. I want you to think about me. Stop trying to be something that you're not. It costs too much. People have choices. They can do Shakespeare. They can play golf.

(CHRISSIE *has no real idea why she is feeling what she's feeling. She will slip the stub into her Levi's shorts pocket.*)

CHRISSIE: . . . This is so weird.

CANTRELL: . . . What do you mean?

CHRISSIE: This is just so weird. That's all!

(CHRISSIE *does something, does its opposite, does the first thing again.* CANTRELL *watches her.*)

CANTRELL: . . . What seems weird?

CHRISSIE: Fuck off! Just fuck off! Who do you think you are? . . . One of my foster fathers?!

CANTRELL: What seems weird?

CHRISSIE: Just shut up!

CANTRELL: If you want to leave—then leave.

CHRISSIE: No!

CANTRELL: Stay, then.

CHRISSIE: God! You have . . .

(CHRISSIE *hits or throws something.*)

No one gives me presents! Do you know that?! *No* one! You have really fucked up my life! You have really fucked up my life tonight—*badly!*

(CANTRELL *stares at her.* CHRISSIE *takes off one of her sandals and throws it at him.*)

Shit!

(CANTRELL *moves to where he's put his fridge on the bureau.* CHRISSIE *stares at him, in part afraid he's going to do something violent.* CANTRELL *opens his fridge, takes out his glass, his vodka, pours himself a drink.*)

. . . So I don't get any?! I'm not here?! I don't get any vodka offered to *me?!*

CANTRELL: Would you like some vodka?

CHRISSIE: No! You stupid asshole. I've got an allergy!

(CANTRELL *puts everything back in place, precisely.*)

My goddamn *real* father—whoever *he* is—gave me all these goddamn allergies! Everything I've got in this fucking world is all *allergies!*

(CHRISSIE *starts crying, throws herself facedown on the bed.* CANTRELL *studies her a moment. He stares out. From his suit coat pocket he produces golf balls. He juggles them, three . . . then four. At some point,* CHRISSIE *looks up from her crying. She stops crying. She watches him.*)

. . . Holy shit.

CANTRELL: I grew up in a carnival.

CHRISSIE: Your parents worked in a carnival?

CANTRELL: I don't know. That's just where I was.

(*It would be ideal if* CANTRELL *could now catch balls behind his back as part of his juggling.*)

CHRISSIE: You . . .

CANTRELL: . . . Young lady?

CHRISSIE: My name is Chrissie.

CANTRELL: I know.

CHRISSIE: You got a bloody rag taped to your hand—and you can still juggle like that?!

CANTRELL: That's the carnival.

(*He juggles.*)

I had a friend in the carnival. We were both your age.

(*He smiles.*)

Thirty-five. Torey Weathers. I haven't had a friend since then. I should get one. Torey had all the jobs that had to do with the hoses. He had hair that was always plastered on his head. Once he hosed down a field where they were going to set up the carnival. I was there. Some . . . like *lightning* jumped from the generator truck to Torey's hose. And Torey . . . rose up. He . . . lifted up . . . like he was something that the hose was juggling. I ran and turned off the generator. And Torey came down. He didn't die. That night, Torey and I ate pizza together. I have three knives I'd stolen from Rizcatto, the knife thrower. Torey said to me, "I'm the Loch Ness Monster! . . . I'm the Loch Ness Monster!"

> (CANTRELL *smiles at the memory.*)

CHRISSIE: You're in space.

> (CANTRELL *nods.*)

. . . So close the curtain.

> (CANTRELL *mimes the closing of his motel room curtain.*)

. . . Flip the lights.

> (*A beat.* CANTRELL *flips the lights.* CHRISSIE *lifts her tank top off. Under it she wears a cheap satin bra.*)

CANTRELL: What's that?

CHRISSIE: What's what?

CANTRELL (*indicating—by his own shoulder blades*): On your skin. The pink. Like tiny flowers.

CHRISSIE: It's my allergies. It's my goddamn allergies, stupid. How can you see them? It's dark.

CANTRELL: Training.

CHRISSIE: Shit!

> (*Silence.* CANTRELL *doesn't move.*)

So . . . ?

CANTRELL: . . . Excuse me. What's the question?

CHRISSIE: Listen . . . you're a big boy. You've lived in Las Vegas. You know what's going on. You know what to do.

> (CANTRELL *crosses to his bureau. He picks up two ends of a towel that is there with something in it and carefully carries it across, setting it down on the bed. He shines a penlight onto it.*)

What's that?

CANTRELL: What does it look like?

CHRISSIE: . . . It looks like . . . all the parts of your gun.

CANTRELL: It's my instrument.

CHRISSIE: What do you mean . . . it's your "instrument"? It's your *gun*.

CANTRELL: It's all the parts of my instrument—broken down.

CHRISSIE: Yeah . . . *gun* pieces.

CANTRELL: Remember that.

CHRISSIE: Remember what?

CANTRELL: About the world . . . That everything in the world is just pieces—added up. . . . Parts . . . Parts . . . I could juggle these . . . and entertain people.

(*Pause.*)

CHRISSIE (*touching* CANTRELL'*s arm with her hand, running her finger*): So . . .

(*A beat.*)

CANTRELL: No.

CHRISSIE: No?

CANTRELL: No.

CHRISSIE: Why? What do you mean . . . "No."

CANTRELL: I mean . . . "No." I jerk off in the shower. Put your sweater back on.

(*Blackout. Music. As smooth and swift a transition as possible. Light coming up on the golf course.*)

CHRISSIE: This game sucks!

(*Light up now.* CHRISSIE *and* CANTRELL *on the course—* CHRISSIE *with club.*)

CANTRELL: Try it again.

CHRISSIE: I'm telling you, this game sucks! I hate it!

(CANTRELL *points to where we imagine a ball.* CHRISSIE *swings. They both watch the ball soar.*)

CANTRELL: Nice shot.

CHRISSIE (*proud*): Pretty good—huh?

CANTRELL: Excellent.

CHRISSIE: Not bad—for a little slut of a brat like me.

(CANTRELL *stares at her hard, reproachfully.*)

So . . . are you, you know . . . thinking about, like, *confessing?* You know, like . . . turning yourself in?

(CANTRELL *is balancing a five iron on his chin.*)

CANTRELL: Why?

(*He adds a two iron.*)

Why? . . . Why do that? What's the future?

CHRISSIE: . . . I don't know.

(CANTRELL *throws his chin into the air. The clubs rise. He catches them. He mimes putting a ball down. He addresses it. He swings.* CHRISSIE's *eyes grow wide.*)

. . . God, you're so fucking good! . . . How'd you get so fucking good so fast?

CANTRELL: Concentration.

CHRISSIE: I think it's fucking amazing!

CANTRELL: Don't say that word so much.

CHRISSIE: . . . You could go on television. You could be a pro.

CANTRELL: If you're going to do something with your life—you should do it. I'm playing golf. I don't want to go on television.

CHRISSIE: Why not? Those guys make money!

CANTRELL: I've done that. I've made money. That's history. I went to Shakespeare last night.

CHRISSIE: Uh-*uh*.

CANTRELL: "Uh-*uh*"? What do you mean . . . "uh-*uh*"?

CHRISSIE: I mean . . . you didn't go. You couldn't have. It isn't open yet.

CANTRELL: I went to watch it rehearse. A woman let me.

CHRISSIE: So did it suck?

CANTRELL: You use a lot of words that end with those three letters.

CHRISSIE: Well . . .

CANTRELL: It was *Richard the Third.* That's what they said. . . . I don't know. I think Shakespeare needs, maybe, to change his life. At the end . . . the end of the play, this guy, this Richard . . . the Third—I never saw the first two; I don't know *where* they were—he comes out, and he says, "My kingdom for a horse!" Then he says it again. Then someone else comes in . . . with a sword . . . and kills him. And this other guy says, "The bloody dog is dead!"

CHRISSIE: . . . So . . .

CANTRELL: So I don't know . . . horses and dogs . . . horses and dogs. The guys were animals. . . . Then, at the *very* end, the same guy, the guy who hit Richard, says, "God say amen!" And somebody, somewhere in the place, did a number on a trumpet. . . . Here—I'm going to use one of your words: Fuck that life! You know? I *did* that. People saying, "God say amen," after they hit people. I'm sorry. I'm not doing Shakespeare. Shakespeare needs to play golf.

(*To* CHRISSIE.)

Put your club on my hand there.

(*She puts her club on the extended fingertips of one of his hands.*)

Good. Thank you. Now put *my* club on my other hand.

(*She does.*)

Thank you.

(CANTRELL *balances both clubs.*)

. . . "Replica" . . . "Replica" . . .

(*The lights fade. Country-and-western music. Dim light on one of the* COWBOYS *at the bar. Fade in the sound of at least one car honking on a street.*)

RUPERT'S VOICE: I'm not movin'! . . . I'm not movin'! Go ahead! Why don't you just drive on over me, asshole—with your fucking Seville!

(*Light up at the front of the playing area, center.* RUPERT, *a hairy and unruly man in a Hawaiian shirt, down vest, khaki pants, and combat boots, faces his wheelchair into the car seat that* CANTRELL *used in the early scenes. He is kicking with his boots at the front of the "car." Lights also up on* CANTRELL, *eating at bar/café table. He is hearing the ruckus outside. By the time* RUPERT *is through,* CANTRELL *will be outside.*)

RUPERT: No! I *won't* move. No, I won't move, man—tough shit! . . . Hey! Hey—I went to fucking *Nam* for you, man. I slept with fucking snakes! I fucked my body up with *chemicals!* Charlie took my *legs!* You got some extra legs for me? You got some legs you want go give me, Rich-man? For doing that for you? For puttin' my life on the line for you? I'm a fucking *hero,* man! I'm a fucking crippled *hero.* Get your Seville out of my way!

(CANTRELL *takes the back of* RUPERT'S *wheelchair and starts to wheel him out of the "road."*)

CANTRELL: Let's go.

RUPERT: Hey! What the fuck do you . . . ?!

CANTRELL: Light just turned green.

RUPERT: Watch it, man!

CANTRELL: I'm saving your life. It's a dangerous intersection.

RUPERT: All right, Jerko!—you got warned!

(*From somewhere,* RUPERT *produces a piece of metal tow cable and swings it at* CANTRELL. *It strikes* CANTRELL *on the face. In a flash,* CANTRELL *has grabbed the cable and has it tight around* RUPERT'S *neck.* CANTRELL *and* RUPERT *face directly into the audience. We should see* CANTRELL'*s cracked-open face, and the thread by which* RUPERT'*s life hangs.*)

CANTRELL (*very calmly*): I would like to say something. I would like to give you some information, it's important. This is nothing for me. This is like watching television . . . or driving up and ordering a Quarter Pounder and fries. You see—your head is just a head—that's all. It's just a head; it's just another head. And I've kept three heads in the air. At one time. Like medicine clubs . . . Same time—balanced someone's cock on my chin. But the point is . . . the point is, you see—the carnival's over. The carnival's over, Jack. It left town. Yesterday. So the both of us . . . need to remember that. Especially you.

(CANTRELL *relaxes the cable on* RUPERT'*s neck. He removes it.* RUPERT, *wide-eyed, turns to look at* CANTRELL. CANTRELL *nods to him.*)

Get a job as a receptionist. You could excel. Give up kicking cars and excel at the trade of receptionist. I feel confident that you could do it. You just need to apply yourself.

(*Silence. Tableau. Fade light. The ringing of* CANTRELL'*s motel telephone. Dim light on* THE MAN *in a suit at a public phone.*)

Yes?

MAN: Cantrell?

CANTRELL: Hello?

MAN: Cantrell?

CANTRELL: Hello?

MAN: You know—I don't know a person likes to work as hard as I had to work to *find* you.

(*Light, by now, up on* CANTRELL *in his motel room.* CHRISSIE *is in the room, trying to juggle two golf balls. Every time one drops, she says, "Fuck!"*)

. . . Cantrell?

CANTRELL: Hello?

MAN: I said—I don't know a person likes to work as hard as I . . .

CANTRELL: Hard work's good for everyone.

MAN: They say you take assignments. You do work.

CANTRELL: I took my name out of the yellow pages.

MAN: I've got an assignment.

CANTRELL: I'm out of business. I lost my lease. I had my "prices slashed to rock bottom" last week.

MAN: I don't think so.

CANTRELL: Well, then read it over one more time, and you can take the quiz again tomorrow—I'm out of business. I lost my . . .

MAN: From what *I* hear . . . you can't *afford* to be out of the assignment business. I hear—anyone gets out, people start to worry. People start to worry . . . then the assig*nor* gets to be the assig*nee*. You understand what I'm saying?

CANTRELL: . . . Call up Shakespeare.

MAN: Listen, Cantrell—I'm calling from a pay phone on Paradise Road. I don't have a lot of spare change in my pocket to bullshit and humor you.

CANTRELL: I'm in golf now. I'm in doglegs and traps.

MAN: You're in the *ground*, smart guy! That's where *you're* going!

(THE MAN *hangs up. Light fades on his phone.* CANTRELL *hangs up.*)

CHRISSIE: Who was that?

CANTRELL: Used car salesman. He wants me to trade in my Audi.

CHRISSIE: Are you ever serious?

(CANTRELL *doesn't answer.*)

. . . Why won't you tell me how that (*indicating his slashed face*) happened?

(CANTRELL *is looking out the window.* RUPERT *is there, in a pool of light, in his wheelchair.*)

CANTRELL: Looks like the golf course is "under siege."

CHRISSIE: You're *insane.*

CANTRELL: Looks like golf may be tougher than I thought.

CHRISSIE: What're you talking about?

CANTRELL: Just the pieces.

CHRISSIE: Why won't you tell me what happened?

CANTRELL: You don't like my face?

CHRISSIE: I think it's *ugly!*

CANTRELL: I had it sewed up—just for you. Should I take the stitches out?

CHRISSIE: No! Yich! Come on—what happened?

CANTRELL: I was in the library—a book bit me. That's where I read those words "under siege." Like them?

CHRISSIE: I think someone forgot to lock your door!

(*The phone rings again. Dim light on* THE MAN *at the public phone.*)

You're popular!

CANTRELL: How's the juggling coming?

CHRISSIE: It's stupid! I'm terrible! When're you going to fuck me, anyway?

CANTRELL (*pointing to the golf balls on the bed*): Practice.
(*Answering.*)
Yeah.

MAN: Cantrell?

CANTRELL: Here we go again. Hello?

MAN: Cantrell—I'm gonna give you one more chance. I have an assignment. It's forty thousand. Guy who's skimmed quarter of a mil in black chips over the last year. From a baccarat pit. At the Trop. And we both know that that's not in the rulebook. So . . . the access is nothing. No risk. Piece of cake. You take the assignment . . . or I call someone else and give them *two* assignments. Are we clear about what's being described here?

CANTRELL: . . . Is this the guy who keeps saying, "My kingdom for a horse"?

MAN: Cantrell—what're you talking about?

CANTRELL: I'd use a six iron.
(CANTRELL *hangs up.*)

MAN: Cantrell?! . . . Asshole! . . . All right . . . !
(*Blackout phone and* THE MAN'*s light.*)

CANTRELL (*to* CHRISSIE): You know what I learned this morning? In the library? I learned the following things: One—"Methyl salicylate, occurring naturally as wintergreen oil, is the most widely used counterirritant." Two—"The right lens for a man prowling at dusk for moody pictures of wildfowl in swamps will have to be a fast one in order to provide him with enough light to make his pictures." Three . . .

CHRISSIE: Stop it! I mean it—stop that shit—it scares me! You can get so fucking off the wall that it isn't funny! And it scares me. I mean—why are you telling me these things?! Why are you going to the library and learning that shit!

CANTRELL: It's interesting.

CHRISSIE: Yeah, well . . .

CANTRELL: I never finished school. I never went to the library. Now I'm doing both.
(CHRISSIE *sulks.*)
I'm sorry if I scared you.
(*Silence.* CANTRELL *goes to his bureau, gets a small gift-wrapped box, and brings it to* CHRISSIE.)

CHRISSIE (*in her sulking*): I don't even know why I talk to you. You are the most weird fucking man I have ever met.

CANTRELL: So how's my hand?

CHRISSIE: Your what?

CANTRELL: My hand.

CHRISSIE: It's not your hand! Your hand's still *on* you, stupid! It's your finger.

CANTRELL: How's my finger?

(CHRISSIE *doesn't answer.*)

How's my finger?

CHRISSIE: I had it outside on a rock. A dog got it. I *hate* that dog. I chased that dog for a year and finally got it. It's pretty much bone.

(CANTRELL *brings the small white box out from behind his back.*)

CANTRELL: Don't look that way.

CHRISSIE: What's that?

CANTRELL: Open it.

CHRISSIE: What is it?

CANTRELL: It's whatever it is.

(CHRISSIE *takes the box, opens it, removes a gold chain, holds it up. In spite of herself, as usual, she is moved.*)

It's got the name of the jewelry store. On the top of the box. The guy will put the bone on. . . . It's like Indian jewelry. It's all set up.

CHRISSIE: . . . I told my mother I was dating a forty-three-year-old guy who'd killed forty-seven people and cut his finger off and given it to me. She didn't believe me. She sees that bone on this chain, she'll freak out.

CANTRELL: What's your mother do?

CHRISSIE: She's a receptionist. . . . J.B.'s Big Boy.

(CANTRELL *walks to where he can look out and see* RUPERT *again.*)

CANTRELL: "Cedar City, Utah!"

CHRISSIE: Yeah—la-di-da! That's where we are!

CANTRELL: I wonder what ever happened to my friend Torey Weathers. I wonder where he would be. Where he lives. If he's alive. What he's doing. If he remembers flying at the end of the carnival hose.

CHRISSIE: Would you take me somewhere?

CANTRELL: Where?

CHRISSIE: It's a great place to drive. It's by Brian Head. It's called "Cedar Breaks."

CANTRELL: "Cedar Breaks."

CHRISSIE: It's, like, this hundred-mile-high *cliff.*

(CANTRELL *nods. He's watching* RUPERT. CHRISSIE *holds up her chain.*)

Thank you.

CANTRELL: Right.

CHRISSIE: Thank you, Cantrell.

(*Fade the light. Hold the light a beat longer on* RUPERT; *have him wheel himself out of it. Cross-fade the sound of a car on the road, the car radio playing low. Cross-fade that after some beats with night sounds. Fade in dim, moonish light on overlook area. And on* CANTRELL'S *car: same light.* CANTRELL *and* CHRISSIE *are staring far out and away.*)

CANTRELL: . . . "Scenic Overlook."

CHRISSIE: This is so fucking cosmic! . . . "E.T.—Phone home!"

(CHRISSIE *laughs.* CANTRELL *opens his door.*)

Where're you going?

CANTRELL: To the edge.

CHRISSIE: Wait!

(CHRISSIE *opens her door and joins* CANTRELL. *They walk together to the guardrail. They stand there.* CHRISSIE *is hugging* CANTRELL'S *waist. Several beats in silence.*)

. . . See that light?

(*Pointing.*)

Hundred and thirty miles! No shit. From an oxide plant. This guy my mother saw worked there. They got so many, I heard, what-they-call *fossil fuels* in all this stuff, this place—if you *lit* them, you could lift the whole fucking planet like a rocket. Why don't you want to lay me?

CANTRELL: . . . You know what I think?

CHRISSIE: Why don't you want to lay me, Cantrell?

CANTRELL: I think . . . that if your mind was strong enough . . . you could juggle yourself. . . . You could just . . . jump over this railing here. And juggle yourself. Keep yourself in the air. And never fall.

(CANTRELL *makes the juggling motions with his hands.*)

CHRISSIE: . . . I told this girl I know . . . Crystal? she's almost a friend . . . that I had a lover. I said my lover killed people. I said he was a criminal.

CANTRELL: I'm not a criminal.

CHRISSIE: Really. Tell me about it.

CANTRELL: I'm not a criminal. Criminals are bad. I'm not a bad person.

(*A beat.* CHRISSIE *stretches and kisses* CANTRELL *on his suture.*)

CHRISSIE: I know.

CANTRELL: I have an entertainer's heart.

CHRISSIE: I know.

CANTRELL: Once . . .

CHRISSIE: . . . "Once" . . . ?

CANTRELL (*saying it for himself, looking straight and far out*): I have an entertainer's heart.

CHRISSIE: I can't figure you.

CANTRELL: One time . . . I pulled three people from a rolled-over "Z." It was on the Tonopah Highway . . . and I broke the back windshield with a rock. And I pulled the three people out. . . . It was two men and a woman. Twenties. One guy was dead. The other two were alive. It was dark—like now. Raining. The one guy who was alive was saying, "It wasn't me . . . it wasn't me," . . . but his voice was . . . something was in the way of his voice. He wasn't conscious. The girl was out too; she wasn't saying anything. The dead guy I rolled over into a gully—he was dead. The other two . . . I took their clothes off to see if there were bad places that they were bleeding. On the girl, something had gone into her chest. So I ripped my shirt and did the best I could—stopping the blood. I keep a blanket in my Audi. I just keep it. I wouldn't drive without a blanket. So I wrapped the two, the guy still saying in his voice that something was in the way of, "It wasn't me," and I got them back to a truck stop south of Austin. I'm not a bad person. When I was thirteen, thumbing in California near the border, this guy who said, "I own three casinos," picked me up, then made me suck him off. He held a gun to my head. That pissed me off. It pissed me off for a lot of years. But lately—this week—it's only parts. I can remember it. I can think of it. But it's just . . . pieces. Pieces of what happened . . . at the side of the road: the guy's car—the dust . . . the light . . . his cock . . . my mouth . . . his gun. And all those pieces, even . . . are pieces. Like *my* instrument, now. On the towel. Like you saw. And it doesn't piss me off anymore. It's just . . . pieces of something . . . pieces of pieces . . . pieces of pieces of pieces of all that happened when I was thirteen.

(CANTRELL *takes a deep breath. He stares out.*)

CHRISSIE (*head against his chest*): I can hear your heart beating.

CANTRELL: If you couldn't, I'd be in trouble.

CHRISSIE: It's like a drum.

CANTRELL: No—a *pump*. I read that.

CHRISSIE: Cantrell?

CANTRELL (*spelling*): C-A-N-T-R-E-L-L, Cantrell.

CHRISSIE: Would you kill someone who'd really done a shitty thing to me?

(CANTRELL *doesn't answer. Light up on* RUPERT, *sitting on a barstool, his wheelchair behind him, drinking at the bar.*)

'Cause someone did. . . . And he did it again. And he did it a lot. And it made me feel kind of like . . . puke, you know.

CANTRELL: Like a "cipher." It means "something of no value or importance." "Zero." I learned it yesterday. It means . . .

CHRISSIE (*nodding agreement*): Yeah, and it scared me. And it hurt. He was one of my foster fathers. And I guess—I don't know— maybe I liked it too . . . a little bit. He said I did. Maybe. I don't know. Maybe I'm sick. Maybe he should've killed me or something. Once . . .

(*The phone in* CANTRELL's *motel room starts to ring. Dim outlining light on* THE MAN *at the phone. In the bar we see* RUPERT, *picking up the dead soldiers of beer and hurling them, one after the other, at the bar mirror. We hear the series of shatterings in counterpoint with the phone ringing.*)

MAN: Okay, Bozo . . . ! That's the way you want it, fine!

(*Fade the light on the phone.* RUPERT *emits a bizarre animal roar in the bar.*)

CHRISSIE (*closing out whatever story she's been telling* CANTRELL): So would you do it, Cantrell? Would you kill him?

CANTRELL: Angel . . .

CHRISSIE: Jesus Christ . . . Jesus Christ, Cantrell, I wish you would.

CANTRELL: Honey, I'm out of the business.

CHRISSIE: I know, but . . .

CANTRELL: I'm retired. I told somebody else that, earlier today. I just better not see him *do* anything.

CHRISSIE: Yeah? Well, you *might*. You just might. 'Cause he's still able to. . . . Rupert's still able to do *a lot*. Even in a wheelchair.

CANTRELL: . . . "Rupert?"

CHRISSIE: Rupert!

CANTRELL: "Rupert."

(*Fade the light on* CANTRELL *and* CHRISSIE. *We see* RUPERT, *in the bar. He has been wheeling his chair forward, then back. Now he starts a move that takes him, at first, just outside* CANTRELL's *motel room, where he pauses. Then he moves into it. He waits. Fade the light on* RUPERT. *Music. Fade the light up on* CANTRELL's *car.* CHRISSIE *sits beside* CANTRELL. *She has his blanket around her, rests her head on his shoulder.*)

CHRISSIE: I feel safe with you, Cantrell. Like I'm okay. Like I'm not a . . . what was the word?

CANTRELL: "Cipher."

CHRISSIE: Yeah.

CANTRELL: I need to practice my approach shots.

CHRISSIE: It's so weird. I've never felt safe with anybody before.

CANTRELL: I used to walk out . . . on the Desert Inn Country Club course—five, six A.M.—when the light was like this. The dark. I didn't know why. It was just someplace that felt good. Maybe I knew that I'd stop taking assignments. Maybe I knew that my life would change.

CHRISSIE: . . . We're home.

(CANTRELL *checks beyond the windows of the car apprehensively.*)
We're home. Turn the car off.

CANTRELL: No.

CHRISSIE: "No." Whadda you mean?

CANTRELL: Something's wrong. . . . Something isn't right.

CHRISSIE: Hey, I thought I was spending the night for once!

CANTRELL: The night's over!

CHRISSIE: You bastard!

CANTRELL: Never trust a hit man.

CHRISSIE: You son of a bitch! Goddamn it! I was having a fantasy about us all the way back from Cedar Breaks in the car!

CANTRELL: Look, I just said you could spend the night. I didn't say you could have a fantasy.

CHRISSIE: *You're so fucking weird!*

CANTRELL: Come on.

CHRISSIE: Where're we going?

CANTRELL: It's called a truck stop. You see the trucks? You see them stopped? The trucks are all stopped here for food. This is where they feed the trucks . . . while they're stopped. Sometimes they feed a car too. So that's what we're going to do. We're going to go inside . . . and get fed. It's time for breakfast.

(Reaching into the "back seat," producing a box.)

Oh, and take this with you. Open it when you feel like opening something. Sometimes things need to be opened.

CHRISSIE: What's the matter with you?

CANTRELL: Nothing's the matter with me. I learned another word yesterday. In the library. "Intuition." I'm having an "intuition." This is Cantrell having an "intuition," that's what you're seeing here. Cantrell, stopped at a truck stop, after having had an "intuition." "God say amen!"

CHRISSIE: You need a caretaker.

CANTRELL *(getting out)*: "Thank you, Cantrell. Thank you for the package you just gave me to open." Come on.

CHRISSIE: You need a keeper, who'll come bring food to your cage.

CANTRELL: Good. Now . . . up the stairs . . . and open the door— don't act like a "cipher"—and we'll be in the truck stop. Good. Excellent.

(They are by the café table.)

Good. Now order me an omelette.

(CANTRELL moves off.)

CHRISSIE: So, okay, but what kind of . . . ?!

(But he's gone. The phone starts ringing in CANTRELL's room. RUPERT watches it ring. Finally he picks it up.)

RUPERT: Yeah? . . . Hello?

(We see CANTRELL in a dim light at the pay phone. He hangs up. RUPERT hangs up.)

CANTRELL *(as he strides back to where CHRISSIE sits)*: . . . "Intuition" . . . "Intuition!" . . . "Intuition!" . . .

(Arriving.)

Tricks!

CHRISSIE: I ordered your omelette.

CANTRELL: Somebody thinks they're Einstein!

CHRISSIE: Cantrell?

CANTRELL: Somebody thinks they can teach me lessons. Well, I got my *own* school now! So . . .

CHRISSIE: I ordered your omelette.

CANTRELL: I hate my instrument—do you know that?!

CHRISSIE: Well, I . . .

CANTRELL: I hate it put together. I hate its parts. Tricks! "Intuition"! "Replica," "Rupert," "Cedar City, Utah"! Well, things own their parts. . . . Okay?

CHRISSIE: Sure. Fine. I guess. I don't . . .

CANTRELL: Things own their parts.

CHRISSIE: I ordered your omelette.

CANTRELL: Good. Thank you.

CHRISSIE: You're welcome.

CANTRELL: Now, when it comes—I appreciate it—eat it. I'll be back in an hour.

    (*He leaves.*)

CHRISSIE (*after him*): Cantrell . . . ?!!

    (*Fade to half-light. Music. Phone ringing in* CANTRELL'*s room. Light on* CANTRELL *at the pay phone.* RUPERT *answers the phone.*)

RUPERT: Yeah?

CANTRELL: Cantrell?

RUPERT: Who's calling?

CANTRELL: Cantrell?

RUPERT: Who's calling?

CANTRELL: Cantrell—it's *over* for you.

RUPERT: Hey—maybe this isn't even . . . !

CANTRELL: Your ass is grass. Your blood is mud. Your breath is death.

    (CANTRELL *laughs. Silence.*)

God say amen!

    (CANTRELL *hangs up. The phone starts ringing in the bar.* COWBOY *behind the bar answers it.*)

COWBOY (*across to* CHRISSIE): It's for you!

    (CHRISSIE *runs across to the phone.*)

CHRISSIE: . . . Hello?

CANTRELL: How're you doing?

CHRISSIE: Where *are* you?

CANTRELL: How're you doing?

CHRISSIE: I finished your omelette.

CANTRELL: Good. Excellent!

> (CANTRELL *hangs up. He moves to the center front area, pacing,*
> *gathering himself. As* CHRISSIE *hangs up the phone, the*
> COWBOY *grabs her arm, smiles a shit-eating grin at her.*)

CHRISSIE: Hey, Vern—I mean it—let go.

> (*He doesn't.*)

Let go.

> (*He doesn't.*)

I got friends. I'm a person. I'm not a cipher, so watch out. Let go
of my arm.

> (*A beat. He lets go.* CHRISSIE *crosses back to the table.*)

CANTRELL (*pacing*): . . . Okay . . . Okay. "Methyl salicylate." Hello?
Cantrell? Cantrell, are you listening? Stay alert! Pay attention! If
someone picks up a thirteen-year-old hitchhiker and takes away
some part . . . do you quit the carnival? Pieces! Pieces! Pay
attention, Cantrell! Keep your mind on things! Someone takes
away your balls . . . you juggle clubs. You juggle . . . clubs. Okay.
Good work! Keep your head down! Follow through!
Concentration! Don't look back! Concentration!

> (*In the truck stop, we will see* CHRISSIE *opening her package,*
> *and we will see that it is a white silk scarf with fringe.*
> CANTRELL *moves off to the phone with purpose. Dials. The phone*
> *rings in the motel room.* RUPERT *snatches it up.*)

RUPERT: Hello!

> (*No response.*)

Hello!!

> (*No response.*)

Okay, asshole—who *is* this?!

CANTRELL: Chrissie?

RUPERT: No—this isn't Chrissie.

CANTRELL: You're right! You're on your toes! Good. This is Cantrell.
Himself. Why don't you meet me on the first tee. Of the golf
course. In an hour. My room's a mess.

RUPERT: Your room's not a mess.

CANTRELL: My room's a mess. Take my word for it. There's
somebody there.

RUPERT: It's me.

CANTRELL: Right. Exactly. First tee.

> (CANTRELL *hangs up. Fade his light. Fade* RUPERT'*s light. Light*
> *up slightly on* CHRISSIE, *sitting alone at the table in the café.*)

CHRISSIE (*holding her fork in front of her—a microphone; she feels beautiful draped in her scarf*): . . . And now! . . . The girl you've all been waiting for . . . ! Miss Chrissie Lane! . . . Singing her own rendition for you now of . . . "Motel Memory"!

(*She moves to the juke, plays the song, and gets deeply into singing along as though she were, in fact, the artist.*

This activity should continue throughout the following golf course sequence—as a muted background: CHRISSIE *introducing herself and then singing along with the numbers. One of the numbers, of course, should be "Stand by Your Man." In her self-introductions,* CHRISSIE *should say the following sorts of things in no special order.*)

. . . And now . . . the little girl you've all been hoping to see . . . the girl who's come so much into her own of late . . . And now . . . the girl whose star is clearly on the rise . . . the girl who's rising out of obscurity and is movin' right up the charts . . . Here she is—the girl who's been knockin' 'em all dead in Las Vegas. . . . And now . . . the little gal who's clearly been doin' it *her* way . . . ! Chrissie Lane!

(*On one occasion*)

Crystal Lane!

(*Light up on* CANTRELL *on the golf course. It is a "new"* CANTRELL. *He wears madras pants, a golf shirt, a white visor, golf shoes. He is whistling, perhaps the song that* CHRISSIE *was singing, and practicing his shots.*)

CANTRELL: . . . Elbow straight . . . elbow straight.

(*We see* RUPERT—*hairy and unruly as ever—approaching in his wheelchair. When he is close enough,* CANTRELL *senses his approach, continues his activity without looking up, but speaks.*)

Practicing my approaches.

(RUPERT *takes a squared pistol from the pocket of his down vest.*)

RUPERT: I don't like you with my daughter, man.

CANTRELL: Loft . . . and backspin. Loft . . . and backspin. That's what they tell me. It isn't easy.

(*He takes another shot, is pleased with it.*)

. . . Loft and backspin. It's coming.

(RUPERT *fires—a shot that goes past* CANTRELL. *Nodding to* RUPERT.)

Rupert.

(CANTRELL *smiles, picks up his seven iron and balances it on his chin.*)

"Ru-pert."

RUPERT: Stay . . . the fuck . . . away . . . from Chrissie, man.

(CANTRELL *hikes his chin, sends the seven iron into the air, catches it.*)

CANTRELL: Chrissie tells me stories.

RUPERT: Get someone else!

CANTRELL: With Chrissie's stories?

RUPERT: You had a call, Scarface.

(*Rupert laughs.*)

When I was in your room.

CANTRELL: Right—I called *myself.* I *do* that. Sometimes I answer. Sometimes I don't. But I think it's good. To check in. Don't you? . . . "Ru-pert."

(RUPERT *fires again. This time the shot grazes* CANTRELL's *shoulder.*)

RUPERT: I *hate* that name! I *hate* that name—"Rupert." I hate it!

CANTRELL: Should we play a round? . . . Rupe?

(*From the neon scribble at the back of the set, we see* THE MAN *begin to make a slow approach. He wears the suit and perhaps the hat that we've seen him wearing when he placed his phone calls to* CANTRELL. RUPERT *fires again. This time the shot enters* CANTRELL's *foot.* CANTRELL *makes a sudden, involuntary sound of pain.*)

RUPERT: Guy who called . . . guy who called just said *one* thing, man. Guy said—"One last chance." So I guess that's the fucking message. Right? You understand what I'm saying? I guess that's the fucking message of the morning—"One last chance" . . . for old Cantrell.

CANTRELL: Let me get that down.

(CANTRELL *pulls a tan leatherette notepad from his hip pocket, plucks a golf pencil from his shirt. He is smiling but at the same time wincing.*)

". . . One . . . last . . ." What came next?

RUPERT: You're dead. I was gonna kill you, but . . . you are, I mean, a dead man.

CANTRELL (*writing on his pad*): Just a second. You're going too fast.

RUPERT: You're being *marked.* You're being *hunted.* I saw *The*

Godfather. Someone's on a *strike*, Baby . . . for an asshole named Cantrell. They got their zoom lenses and their scopes looking for a man with a gun.

CANTRELL: Man with a . . . I think that's possible. I think, actually, that's very possible.

RUPERT: Yeah, and, like, very soon.

CANTRELL: How about—just nine holes then? Since time is—how do they say that?—"of the essence"? A dollar a hole. What do you say? "This is the winter of our discontent . . . made summer by the glorious sun of York." . . . Agree? I just learned that. "A horse! . . . A horse! . . . my . . ." Should we get a cart, do you think? Or can we use your wheelchair? A man with a gun. Listen—let me use your wheelchair. You caddy. Disabled's just a state of mind, really—don't you think? Here—you stand. Let me sit. Nine holes. A dollar a hole. I say—we go for it.

(RUPERT *smiles, starts to laugh. He pushes himself, shaking, from the chair, stands on his braces. He nods for* CANTRELL *to sit.* CANTRELL *sits.*)

RUPERT: Now I'm you and you're me.

CANTRELL: Can you feel the grief? Feel the regret? Does it seem a terrible waste to you that you've . . . ?

RUPERT: Hey—now I'm the dude who cools people, man. And you're the schmuck in the chair.

CANTRELL (*with his notepad again*): Excellent! Good! Let me get that down. "Now I'm the . . ." what was it—"dude"?

RUPERT: Yeah—I'm the *dude!* I'm the dude who wastes other people's lives.

CANTRELL: God—your mind is like *lightning!*

RUPERT: And now, baby, you're gonna know just what it feels like—to be a cripple . . . to be "Rupert" . . . 'cause I'm gonna shoot both your fucking kneecaps out. And then I'm gonna leave you for whoever's . . .

CANTRELL: "Now I'm the dude with the gun!" *That* was what you . . .

(THE MAN, *still some distance away, has lifted a gun with a silencer on it. He has fired—each shot a kind of* POP. RUPERT, *with a look of immense surprise on his face, jolts and falls forward over* CANTRELL. CHRISSIE *is still singing and doing her own private routine in the background.* THE MAN *turns and will exit to the back.* CANTRELL *lifts* RUPERT *off and lays him out on the ground. He checks his notepad, reads from it.*)

. . . "One last chance."

(CANTRELL *looks at* RUPERT, *nods.*)

. . . "So, the bloody dog is dead!" . . . "I'm you—you're me." . . . Cantrell is dead. Long live Cantrell. . . . "My kingdom for a horse." "God say amen."

(*The light fades slowly on* CANTRELL *and then slowly on* CHRISSIE, *singing along with the juke in the background. When the light comes up again, it comes up on what was the "overlook" area, upstage right.* CANTRELL *is still in his golf clothes, still in* RUPERT's *wheelchair. There is a police officer with him.*)

OFFICER: Cantrell.

CANTRELL: Cantrell.

OFFICER: Two "l"s?

CANTRELL: Exactly. After a "c" and an "a" and an "n" and a "t" and an "r" and an "e"—two "l"s.

OFFICER: Well, if we need any more information, Mr. Cantrell, we'll call *The Globe.*

CANTRELL: Call the golf course. I'm giving golf my best shot.

OFFICER (*shaking his head*): "Random violence."

CANTRELL: Well . . .

OFFICER: This is not our normal circumstance—that's all I can say. We are not a town known for our random violence.

CANTRELL: Check the Shakespeare. I think maybe . . .

(*In the background, in* CANTRELL's *motel room, we see* CHRISSIE "*dancing*" *to a slow country-and-western song, holding her scarf out like wings.*)

OFFICER: I mean, Rupert was a cruel son of a bitch. Vietnam took his head apart: we could see that. But this kind of sudden thing . . . in broad daylight . . . on a public golf course. . . . I mean—I don't mean to say that everybody here in Cedar City is a saint. Just because it's Utah. Or because our people are LDS, most of them—you know L-D-. . . ?

(*Cantrell nods.*)

But this is not a place where . . .

CANTRELL: Listen . . . uh, my . . .

(*He points to his foot.*)

OFFICER: I mean, Rupert had his . . . do you call them "tics"? . . .

Anyway, "quirks." That was reasonably common knowledge—that he hit women.

CANTRELL: My . . .

OFFICER: He had this . . . it was like a length of tow cable. Did you ever see it? Couple of times we've had to sew up . . . one of the local docs . . . we get reports. And he burned a couple of young girls . . . like with matches, or car cigarette lighters, that stuff.

CANTRELL: My foot, I think, is still . . .

OFFICER: Almost blinded—I guess that *was* pretty bad—this foster daughter of his with a . . . when he was out living with . . . But this random violence that we've got happening around this country . . . and now here. It really makes me want to . . . I mean, I'm not forgiving Rupert for what he was—which was pretty much a kind of local monster. . . . But we all still knew him; he was one of us; this is the town, after all, he'd grown up in . . . been a pretty good tailback for two years, not a bad sixth man off the bench either in the clutch . . . except that, most times, he'd foul out.

(*Shakes his head.*)

I really hate to see this kind of incident come to Cedar City.

CANTRELL: My foot's still bleeding. Could I fix it?

OFFICER: Oh . . . yeah . . . sure. I'm sorry. You told me before. I didn't . . .

CANTRELL: It isn't . . .

OFFICER: When I started the questions. That was Rupert—right?

CANTRELL: Right.

OFFICER: Just before the shots came from behind the bunker.

CANTRELL: Right.

OFFICER: Right. I should've remembered. I should've paid closer attention.

CANTRELL: It was all the random violence, I think . . . distracted you.

OFFICER: . . . You're right.

CANTRELL: I know . . . but I think I've lost a lot of blood.

(*Fast fade of the lights on this scene. Lights up more in the motel. CHRISSIE is putting her piece of jewelry around her neck—bone and all. It makes her feel strangely adult and beautiful. And those feelings confuse her. She sits on the bed. She lies on the bed. She cries there. The country-and-western love song that has been playing cross-fades with the sound track for Three's Company.*)

CANTRELL *approaches the bed from far downstage—from the scribble of neon. His foot is bandaged.*)

. . . It wasn't me. . . . I didn't shoot him. Someone else shot him. . . . It was "random violence." . . . I thought you *wanted* him dead. . . . Are you crying because it actually happened?

CHRISSIE (*Into the bed*): Shut up!

CANTRELL: "Shut up, Cantrell." "You talk too much." "You put your foot in your mouth" . . . although it's harder these days.

CHRISSIE (*Into the bed*): Just keep quiet!

CANTRELL: Jack Tripper just did a forward roll . . . over the couch. You should see it. It's very funny.

(*No response.*)

People stop living when they die. It's amazing that it takes us as long as it takes us, sometimes—maybe I'm just speaking for myself—to realize that . . . Jack Tripper's a funny guy, I think—whatever his name is—not Jack Tripper but the guy who calls himself Jack Tripper in this show. . . . He has an entertainer's heart. . . . You should watch me—I'm juggling three naked women.

(CHRISSIE *looks up fast from her crying.*)

Then I made them disappear. Great trick—huh? If I ever go back to Vegas, I'm going to do warm-up for . . . who? . . . who would be good? . . . Ann-Margret! You like Ann-Margret? You ever seen her? You want me to call her up and have her come over here? She has an entertainer's heart, too. You should see her sweat when she's dancing. You look extremely pretty—wearing that. With the scarf too. You look almost as old as you were trying to be ten days ago when I first met you. You look like someone someone could live a lifetime with. What are you crying about?

(*Silence.* CHRISSIE'*s taking in* CANTRELL'*s barrage.*)

CHRISSIE (*after thinking about it*): Shut up.

CANTRELL: That's good. That's original. That'll be in the library in a couple of hundred years, I'm sure.

CHRISSIE: *I'm confused!!* . . . I'm confused, you stupid off-the-wall asshole! *That's* why I'm crying! I'm confused!

CANTRELL: Good.

CHRISSIE: Yeah—"good." Right. Terrific.

CANTRELL: No—good. You should be. It's a confusing place.

CHRISSIE: *What's* a confusing place?!

CANTRELL: This room. This motel. This world. The television program.

CHRISSIE: You are so fucking weird!

CANTRELL: Some things never change. Be grateful.

CHRISSIE (*slugging him with a pillow*): I'm *mad* at you.

CANTRELL: Why's that, Doll?

CHRISSIE: I just AM!

> (CHRISSIE *hugs the pillow and starts crying into it again.* CANTRELL *rubs her shoulder or strokes her hair.* CHRISSIE *suddenly rips the pillow from in front of her face.*)

BECAUSE FOR A WEEK AND A HALF I'VE WANTED YOU TO TAKE ME TO BED! I'VE REALLY WANTED IT. I'VE REALLY PLANNED ON IT. AND NOW I DON'T WANT YOU TO TAKE ME TO BED ANYMORE! BECAUSE IT'S DIFFERENT! AND IT'S JUST CONFUSING—THAT'S ALL. AND IT MAKES ME MAD!

> (CHRISSIE *collapses again flat on the bed.* CANTRELL *slowly rubs her back. With the fingers of one hand, he traces the suture on his face.*)

CANTRELL: . . . It's just pieces. . . . It's just pieces, honey—that's all. . . . Someday they'll all be in the air . . . and you'll understand. . . . It's just a trick that you have to do . . . using pieces.

> (*Slow fade.*)

The End

Old West

Gus Edwards (1939–) is from the Caribbean (St. Thomas, Virgin Islands). He has been a resident of the United States since 1959. Edwards has studied acting with Stella Adler and at the HB Studios and has studied filmmaking at the New York Institute of Photography. He currently teaches film studies at Arizona State University and lives in Chandler, Arizona. He also runs the Multi-Ethnic Theatre Program. He has twice (1977 and 1979) been an O'Neill Conference playwright. Since then he has had seven plays produced by the Negro Ensemble Company and has written for PBS.

Bartender
a man in his late forties

Boyd
a rugged-looking man in Western clothes; early thirties

Wally
short, overweight; early thirties

Mary
an attractive woman; thirties

Dick
a slim man in a suit; thirties

TIME
The present

PLACE
A roadside bar off a dusty highway running through the desert

(*A bar. The bartender is present when* WALLY *and* BOYD *enter.*)

BOYD: I want to get into some shit. You ever feel in that mood? Drink some liquor, kick some ass, fuck some pussy. Then go on, go home to sleep like a good boy should. You follow?

WALLY: Uh-huh.

BOYD: Barman! Do me something good. Something for a bad dude who feels like drinking some acid and spitting in the face of a grizzly bear.

BARTENDER: What'll it be?

WALLY: Scotch, no chaser. Just a clean glass and some hot whisky.

BARTENDER: You got it.

(*To Boyd.*)

You?

BOYD: Shot 'a bourbon, shot 'a gin, shot 'a vodka, shot 'a rum, shot 'a Southern Comfort all in the same glass with a half 'a glass 'a Coke as a chaser. Just joking. What I look like to you, an idiot? I may be dumb, but I ain't stupid. Give me gin over ice.

BARTENDER: Right.

(*As he goes to make the drinks,* MARY, *a pretty woman in a form-fitting skirt, comes in with* DICK, *dressed in a suit and a tie.*)

BOYD: Well now, lookie, lookie here. See what the desert wind has blown in (*making a sound like the wind*) whooo . . .

(MARY *and* DICK *sit at a table.*)

DICK: What would you like?

MARY: An Alexander.

DICK: Alexander? You sure?

MARY: That's what you asked, and that's what I'd like.

DICK: Okay.

(*He rises.*)

I'll order the drinks, then I'm going to the men's room. Be back in a few minutes.

(MARY *shrugs.* DICK *goes to the bartender.*)

'Scuse me. Er—do you know how to make a Brandy Alexander?

BARTENDER: Uh-huh.

DICK: That's what the lady'll have. I'd like a gin and tonic, in a tall glass.

BARTENDER: You got it.

DICK: Thanks. Er—where's the men's room?

BARTENDER: Out that door and hang a right.

(DICK *goes.*)

BOYD: Boy, I could sure use that in my bed.

WALLY: You ain't the only one. I would even let her use me. How you like them apples?

BOYD: Goddamn, why is it some guys have all the luck? Hey, barkeep! You know the answer to that one?

BARTENDER: I didn't hear you.

BOYD: I was talking to my friend here. Asking him a question. I was saying, "Why is it some guys just seem to have all the goddamn luck?"

BARTENDER: Man, if I knew the answer to that, I wouldn't be stirring drinks. I would be home unraveling the mysteries of life on Planet Earth.

BOYD: I'm sorry I bothered you. Go back to what you were doing.
(*To* WALLY.)
Man is a goddamn fool.

WALLY: You can say that again.

BOYD: I don't want to. I'd rather look at her.
(*Meanwhile,* MARY *at the table is shaking her leg, looking around slightly bored. Finally she rises and goes to the bar.*)

MARY: Excuse me.

BARTENDER: Yes, ma'am?

MARY (*pointing to the jukebox*): That thing work?

BARTENDER: Feed it some quarters, you'll see how good it works.

BOYD: Say, why don't you let me do that?

MARY: Do what?

BOYD: Feed the box some coins, you pick the tunes.

MARY: Why?

BOYD: Because it's the neighborly thing to do, and I'm feeling very, very neighborly.
(WALLY *giggles.*)

MARY: Oh, yeah?

BOYD: Yes, ma'am.

MARY: All right.
(*They go to the jukebox as the* BARTENDER *delivers the drinks to the table.*)
All these tunes are old. Don't they have anything new?

BOYD: Old tunes are the best tunes. Ain't that so, barkeep?

BARTENDER: That's what they tell me.

MARY: Guess I got no choice.

(She punches in a couple.)

Hope you like the songs. After all, it's your money.

BOYD: If you pick 'em, I know I'm going to love them.

MARY: You always like this?

BOYD: How?

MARY: Talk shit to women?

BOYD: Only to the ugly ones. The pigs. To the pretty ones, I bare the secrets of my heart.

MARY: Oh. Well—thanks for the coins.

(She turns to leave.)

BOYD: Say, why don't you let me buy you a drink?

MARY: I already have one. Over there, thank you.

BOYD: Have another. Over here.

MARY: Why?

BOYD: Just to be neighborly. It's the spirit of the old West, you might say.

MARY *(after a moment)*: All right. Just to be neighborly.

BOYD: Atta girl. What'll it be?

MARY *(to the BARTENDER)*: Scotch, no ice. Water chaser.

WALLY: Wowie!

MARY: What's the matter with him?

BOYD: He's a fool. Might even be fucking retarded. Pay him no mind.

(After a beat.)

Brandy Alexander over there, scotch over here, interesting.

MARY: You having trouble with that?

BOYD: Brandy Alexander is a girl's drink.

MARY: And scotch?

BOYD: A woman's. Definitely a woman's drink.

MARY *(offering a toast)*: I'm glad you approve.

(She tosses it back in one gulp.)

BOYD: That ain't all I approve. You want another one?

MARY: No. I better not.

BOYD: Why?

MARY: I'm not alone, as you can see.

BOYD: I thought he was your brother.

MARY: No, we're married. He's my husband.

BOYD: Just passing through?

MARY: Uh-huh.

BOYD: How long you been married?

MARY: Long enough.

BOYD: What's that supposed to mean?

MARY: It means I'd better be getting back.

BOYD: What if I asked you to stay? For the afternoon. For the evening. What the hell, for the whole damn weekend.

MARY: He wouldn't go for it, I can tell you that up front. He would think it was a very bad idea.

BOYD: Suppose I was to explain that I wasn't talking 'bout inviting him. I was talking about us. Just me and you.

MARY: I still don't think he'd like it.

BOYD: Who gives a fuck what he likes? You're the one I'm talking to. What do you like?

MARY: What I like and what I can do are two different things.

BOYD: Tonight let's make them one and the same. Huh?

MARY: I think I'd better not. Excuse me and thanks for the drink.
    (*She returns to her table.*)

BOYD (*to* WALLY): She wants me. That goddamn woman wants me.

WALLY: That's clear to see.

BOYD: And I want her. I want her more than you want your next breath.

WALLY: Well, that's how it works out sometimes.

BOYD: What?

WALLY: A woman wants you. You want her. But somehow or other you can't get together and do something about it. Another time, another place, who knows? Maybe. But here and now — Noooo . . . Been down that road myself. Many times. Many, many times.

BOYD: Shut up.
    (DICK *comes back in, sits.*)

DICK: It's a scorcher out there. This desert heat wilts everything.
    (*Sipping his drink.*)
    Cheers.

BOYD: Four-eyed bastard in a wrinkled suit. Son of a bitch doesn't deserve a woman like that.

WALLY: Hell, no.

BOYD: It's the law of the jungle. Spirit of the old West.

WALLY: What?

BOYD: Survival of the fittest. The strong will prevail.

WALLY: I want another drink.

BOYD: Yeah. Barkeep!

BARTENDER: Right here.

BOYD: Do them again. . . . My goddamn bed was made for a woman like that. You know what I'm saying? You understanding me?

WALLY: So what?

BOYD: So plenty.

WALLY: Come on, let's drink and get out of here. We got a whole night ahead of us.

BOYD: No. Hell, no. Where're we going? What the fuck we going to do? Drive from one town to another, then go home drunk and stupid?

WALLY: Why not? It's as good a way as any to pass the time.

BOYD: No. Not tonight. Only place I'm going is over there. I'm going to take that woman, because I want her.

WALLY: All right. You take her. I'll watch.

(BOYD *gulps his drink, takes a moment to consider, then goes over to the table.*)

BOYD: Excuse me.

DICK: Yes?

BOYD: I want to talk to you.

DICK: Oh, yeah? What about?

BOYD: This woman.

DICK: My wife.

BOYD: Yeah.

DICK: What about her?

BOYD: Well, you see, I desire her, and I think she desires me.

DICK: Oh, yeah?

BOYD: Yes. That's a fact.

DICK: Why don't we ask her?

BOYD: Why don't we keep the lady out of it.

DICK: Is that how "we" doin' things in "these here parts," Cowboy?

BOYD: I got an idea. Why don't you run along. Take the car. I'll see that she gets home safe. Tomorrow.

DICK (*to* MARY): Is this what you were doing while I was away?

MARY: Dick, I don't—

BOYD: Talk to me, Mister. I'm the one you're dealing with. Not the lady, me.

DICK: Don't be a fool, Cowboy. Why don't you leave us alone.

BOYD: I gave you a suggestion, Mister. I think you should follow it.

MARY: Boyd—

BOYD: Keep out of this.

> (*To* DICK.)

Now are you going to leave? Or do I have to make you leave?

DICK: Why are you starting this with me?

BOYD: Yes or no?

DICK: I'm not a violent man.

BOYD: Well, you see, your problem is—I am.

> (WALLY *giggles again.*)

DICK: I still think we should let Mary decide.

BOYD: And I said keep her out of this.

> (*Quickly he kicks the chair from under* DICK, *who falls to the floor.*)

Now you're leaving, because I'm not going home alone tonight. You hear me? And that's a fact. Now let's go.

> (*With that he grabs* DICK *by the collar and jerks him to his feet. As he does, a shot rings out.* BOYD *backs away, holding his stomach.* DICK *is holding a small pistol.*)

Jesus—

> (DICK *fires again.*)

MARY: Dick!

DICK: He assaulted me. You saw it. Everybody did. I had no choice. I'm not a violent man, but I had to protect myself. Isn't that so?

> (BOYD *falls to the floor in a heap.*)

BOYD: Ahhh.

> (*He dies.*)

WALLY: Goddamn . . . Goddamn.

DICK: Is there a doctor around?

BARTENDER: Closest one's about thirty miles away. That's if he's in.

DICK (*to* WALLY): Then it's too late for your friend here.

WALLY: He wasn't no friend. Not really. I hardly knew the man, to tell you the truth. It may've looked like we were together, but we weren't No, sir. I . . . I didn't know him at all.

DICK (*to the* BARTENDER): I don't know what you're going to tell the police.

BARTENDER: Sheriff's even further away than the doctor. But I'm going to tell him what happened. Exactly as I seen it.

DICK: That's fine. And fair. There's only one problem: I can't wait for the sheriff. We've got to get going. Got a lot of ground to cover. Ain't that so, Hon?

MARY: Yes. Yes, we do.

BARTENDER: I know how that can be. If a man's got to go, the man's got to go.

DICK: What do I owe you for these drinks?

BARTENDER: Hundred bucks apiece. Cash. No traveler's checks.

DICK: Sounds reasonable. What about this man here? Looks like he could use a drink. Here's another hundred. Buy him one.
(*Takes out some bills, tosses them on the table.*)

WALLY: Thanks—Mister.

DICK (*to* MARY): You okay?

MARY: I'm—fine.

DICK: Let's go.
(*They exit.*)

WALLY: What'd you think's going to happen when the sheriff gets here?

BARTENDER: How the hell should I know? I'm just a bartender, remember.
(BARTENDER *picks up the money* DICK *left on the table.*)

WALLY: When you going to call him?

BARTENDER: The sheriff? . . . Oh—'bout an hour or so. No need to hurry. Man might be doing something he don't want to be disturbed from. . . . You want the same thing you was drinking before?

WALLY: Yeah. Why not.

BARTENDER: Maybe I'll join you. Mind if I do?

WALLY: No. Glad to have the company.
(BARTENDER *pours two drinks, from which they both take big gulps.*)

BARTENDER: Now, what were you saying before you were so rudely interrupted?

WALLY: Talking about the old West and about how much it's changed.

BARTENDER: Oh, yeah, that's what we were talking about, wasn't it?

WALLY: Yeah—that's what it was. Cheers.
(*They click glasses.*)
(*Music comes up; lights fade.*)

The End

JULIE JENSEN

The Total Meaning of Real Life

Julie Jensen (1942–) was raised in Beaver, Utah, and was the 1959 St. George Rodeo Queen. Her first full-length play, *Cisterns,* premiered at the Attic Theatre in Detroit. Early one-acts were produced at the Negro Ensemble Company, the Quaigh Theatre, and at the Women's Project. Jensen's *Stray Dogs* won the CBS/Dramatists Guild Prize and opened at Arena Stage; it is published by Dramatists Play Service. Her *White Money* won the 1990 Award for New American Plays and premiered at the Salt Lake Acting Company; she directed a 1993 production of this play at the Powerhouse Theatre in Los Angeles, earning a nomination for Best Play of 1993 from *LA Weekly. The Total Meaning of Real Life* is from Jensen's *The Lost Vegas Series.* Her plays have been published in *Alaska Quarterly Review, Kenyon Review,* and *The Literary Review.* In early 1994, she was playwright-in-residence at Thurber House at Ohio State University. And later in 1994 she became head of the M.F.A. playwriting program at the University of Nevada, Las Vegas.

The Total Meaning of Real Life was first
produced as a part of an evening of one-acts
by Playwrights in Exile at the Rubie Theatre
in Los Angeles, August 12, 1993, and directed
by Cliff Fennerman.

CHARACTERS
Girl

Creepy Guy

TIME
The present

PLACE
A wedding chapel in Las Vegas
There's a suggestion of a tiny chapel onstage. It's romantically lit, but there is a distinct and obvious cheapness about it.

(GIRL *enters from up left, outside the chapel. She's wearing a pair of clear plastic heels decorated with rhinestones, a tight—very tight—black miniskirt, and an oversized black Levi's jacket. Her hair is dyed black, obviously dyed, and disheveled. A bag is slung over her shoulder.*)
(*She walks across the back of the stage, then straight toward the audience.*)

GIRL: It is a perfectly normal night in Vegas. Hot and dry and smelling like someone's been sick. I'm on my way to commit suicide.

(*She stops and lights a cigarette.*)

I'm heading north on Las Vegas Boulevard toward Freemont Street. The lights up ahead make the horizon look like a war zone. I pass a quick marriage chapel called Wee Kirk. Wee Kirk O the Heather. It's sandwiched between two dirty bookstores and another marriage joint called The Hitchin' Post, which has a western theme. Wee Kirk, Wee Kirk O the Heather—it's got a theme of Scotland.

(*She indicates the church.*)

Since I'm on my way to commit suicide anyway, I figure I'll drop in. Get myself some pastoral counseling. And Wee Kirk, Wee Kirk O the Heather is open. It's always open, it says.

(*She drops her cigarette, steps on it, and walks inside.*)

I walk on in. The place looks like it was made by Keebler elves. Yo ho ho, anybody home?

(*Silence.*)

This creepy guy twirls out of the darkness wearing green bell-bottoms and a sequin bow tie.

(CREEPY GUY *appears. He's short, plump, and sweaty.*)

He's got a perpetual grin like an idiot child left out in front of the monkey cage.

CREEPY GUY: Name, please.

GIRL: The question takes me by surprise.

(*She smiles at the* CREEPY GUY, *looks around and picks her name off the sign.*)

Heather.

CREEPY GUY: Last name.

GIRL: Kirk.

(*To audience*): He eyes me. You can tell he don't believe me. So he starts all over again.

CREEPY GUY: *Real* name.

GIRL (*she waits, then grins at him*): Mitzi.

CREEPY GUY: Last name.

GIRL: Gaynor.

But that don't seem to satisfy him either. He tells me he's got something he wants me to know.

CREEPY GUY (*closes the book he's writing in*): I've got just one thing.

GIRL: Yeah.

CREEPY GUY: One thing to tell you.

GIRL: What's that?

CREEPY GUY: Everybody's somebody.

GIRL: Everybody's something, he says. And he closes the book he's been writing in. He starts in, then, like he's a recorded message from the phone company.

CREEPY GUY (*delivered in mannered, memorized way*): Welcome to Wee Kirk. Wee Kirk O the Heather. Built in 1940, it *is* one of the oldest wedding chapels *in* Las Vegas. Over sixty-five thousand couples have been united *in* the holy bonds of matrimony with*in* our chapel. Would you like a brochure *of* our services?

GIRL: No thanks, I say. But I take one anyway.

(*Pauses.*)

He's standing behind a little pulpit that looks like a Walt Disney doghouse. And behind him is a wall of wedding bouquets under glass.

CREEPY GUY: Wee Kirk O the Heather features a choice *of* five different wedding packages *for* your convenience, starting *with* the supersaver, which includes *a* carnation bouquet . . .

GIRL: And he points to the smallest and plainest of the bouquets under glass.

CREEPY GUY: . . . *Three* wallet-sized wedding photos . . .

GIRL: And he points to an index card on the wall.

CREEPY GUY: . . . And *a* complimentary wedding garter.

GIRL: Then he slides back the roof of the doghouse. Inside is a bunch of blue garters. Which he digs his hands into like they're autumn leaves.

CREEPY GUY: Our supersaver *is* regularly $129.95, marked down *this* week to $109.95. Would you like to examine the garters?

GIRL: No. No thanks, I say, I just came in here to get some pastoral counseling.

CREEPY GUY: Some what?

GIRL: Some pastoral counseling.

CREEPY GUY: I'm afraid we don't offer that here. We *do,* however, have a special this month on the deluxe matrimonial, complete *with* live organ music, *the* minicascade of roses bouquet, *an* imitation wood frame *for* your license, and a videotape *of* the complete ceremony. Of course, all ceremonial packages *do* come *with* the complimentary wedding garter.

GIRL: Again he plunges his hand into the garters.

CREEPY GUY: Could I interest you in that?

GIRL: No, I don't think so today. I'm on my way to kill myself.

CREEPY GUY: That matrimonial deluxe also comes—this week *only*—*with* a complimentary wedding breakfast *at* the all-you-can-eat Chuck-o-Rama.

GIRL: Sounds tasty. But it'd just be a waste of food for me.

CREEPY GUY (*in an exaggerated singsong*): Begin each *and* every day
In *a* hearty, healthy way.
And no matter *what* you have to do,
It will *go* just that much easier for you.

GIRL: Up to and including killing yourself?
(*Pause.*)
He just grins and nods at me. We're both waiting for something.
He's wearing hundred percent pure polyester.

CREEPY GUY: So, tell me, Mitzi Gaynor, . . . where *are* you going to do it?

GIRL: At the Golden Nugget, I tell him.

CREEPY GUY: I once saw someone die in the Golden Nugget.

GIRL: Lucky you.

CREEPY GUY (*whispering*): His family got a great deal of money from the casino not to tell anyone where it happened.

GIRL (*shrugs*): I just shrug. Don't say nothing.

CREEPY GUY: A *great* deal of money.

GIRL: Right away I can tell what he's thinking. He's thinking that if he can marry me before I commit suicide, he'll stand to make a great deal of money, a *great* deal of money.

CREEPY GUY: So, tell me, Mitzi Gaynor, have you ever been to Hawaii?

GIRL: Yeah, I been to Hawaii.

CREEPY GUY: You can go there tonight with our special Hawaiian wedding luau, complete *with* genuine grass skirt, flower lei, and the sound track *from* the motion picture *Blue Hawaii*, starring *the* King himself, Elvis Presley.

(*The Elvis Presley version of "I Want You, I Need You, I Love You" begins playing. The* CREEPY GUY *twirls out from behind the pulpit. He lip-syncs the song, doing a terribly serious imitation of Elvis. He jumps and prostrates himself in front of her.*)

"I want you, I need you, I love you
With all my heart."

(*An instrumental interlude plays. He waltzes with the* GIRL; *then he speaks with his own voice, still imitating Elvis.*)

"You know . . . a wise man once said . . . it's not what you take from this life . . . but what you give . . . and you know . . . I feel that way tonight."

(*They twirl.*)

"I feel . . . I feel I wanna give you something tonight."

(*Another twirl. The music stops. He continues to hold her.*)

What do you say, little darlin'?

GIRL: Thanks anyway, but I'm pretty set on killing myself.

(*He returns to the pulpit.*)

CREEPY GUY: I guess you don't know who I am, do you?

GIRL: A creepy little guy hawking ten-minute weddings at Wee Kirk O the Heather. That ain't enough for you?

CREEPY GUY: This is just a disguise. I'm actually someone else.

GIRL: Everybody's somebody.

CREEPY GUY: But they're pretending. I'm for real.

GIRL: Right.

CREEPY GUY: Can *you* guess who I really am?

GIRL: Well, you sure as hell ain't Elvis Presley.

CREEPY GUY: No.

GIRL: And you ain't Wayne Newton.

CREEPY GUY: No. I'm Randolph Scott!

GIRL: You're not Randolph Scott.

CREEPY GUY: I'm Randolph Scott, star of a hundred and eighty-six major motion pictures, including *Gunfighter, Gun for Hire, Guns at Dawn, Guns across the Sky,* and *Guns in Your Face.*

GIRL: "*Guns in Your Face*"?

(CREEPY GUY *twirls out from behind his podium, unbuttons his jacket, grabs a six-shooter from his belt, twirls it, and shoots straight up.*)

CREEPY GUY: *Guns in Your Face.* I'm Randolph Scott.

GIRL (*to audience*): I look at him. Randolph Scott was the strong but vacant type, I say.

CREEPY GUY: Randolph Scott was the father of us all.

GIRL: Yeah, but Randolph Scott was over six feet tall.

CREEPY GUY: Randolph Scott was five foot six. He played all his scenes on a box.

GIRL: That was Alan Ladd. You got yourself mixed up with Alan Ladd.

CREEPY GUY: I had it out with Alan Ladd.

(*He runs up the aisle, pistol drawn. He hides behind a pew and shoots at the altar. Then he runs to the altar, guarding it. When he gets at point-blank range, he shoots. The altar falls over.*)

I shot Alan Ladd. He lay crumpled and bleeding at my feet. And then he rose up on his arm, a small trickle of blood dripping from the corner of his mouth. He had a pleading look in his eyes. "Please shoot me again," he begged. "Please shoot me again." But I would not shoot him again. He died in agony at my feet.

(CREEPY GUY *jumps up behind the altar, watching a dying man at his feet.*)

He died waiting for me. Waiting for me to plug him again.

GIRL: Must have been a lovely moment for you both.

(CREEPY GUY *steps up on the altar, then jumps down off it and comes toward the* GIRL *with a swagger.*)

CREEPY GUY: Oh, I've had it out with the best of them. I've had it out with John Wayne. Yes, I duked it out with the Duke. Twenty-two minutes of jam-packed, rock 'em, sock 'em western action.

(*He demonstrates as he's speaking.*)

I hit him a hundred and six times with my bare fists. I knocked him down a set of stairs, I broke a chair over his head, and I threw him through a plate-glass window.

GIRL: And you felt so much the better afterwards.

CREEPY GUY: And now here *you* are. Mitzi Gaynor, perky, plucky, peppy Mitzi. Just as giddy as Kansas in August. High as a kite on the Fourth of July.

(*He trains his gun on her and paraphrases the chorus from Rodgers's and Hammerstein's "I'm in Love with a Wonderful Guy" to lavish orchestral accompaniment.*)

"... she's in love,
she's in love with a wonderful guy."

GIRL: Look, Randolph, you've done a good show, but you're making me tired.

CREEPY GUY: I want you for my wife. I want to plug you again and again.

GIRL: I got no damn time for that. And I've also changed my mind about the pastoral counseling. I'm just gonna get the hell outta here.

CREEPY GUY: Not so fast, Dolly.

(*Training the gun on her.*)

I want you. I need you.

GIRL: Well, you can't have me. Now give me that gun. You're crazy as a chain saw.

(*He shoots the bag from her shoulder.*)

CREEPY GUY: Mitzi. Wipe that cheery expression off your face. Wipe that bubbly optimism from your demeanor. We're serious here. We're deadly serious.

GIRL: You don't get it, Randolph. You can't threaten me. I'm on my way to commit suicide.

(*She slowly folds her hands and then quickly, like a cowboy, she hits his forearm. The gun falls to the floor.*)

Now I just wanna walk quietly out of here, progress on up the street, buy myself a roll of quarters, set out a bottle of Valium, order a bourbon straight up, and play out my quarters.

(*She picks up the gun.*)

And I want you to stay the hell out of my way.

CREEPY GUY: They ain't no bullets in that gun.

GIRL: Randolph Scott never ran out of bullets.

CREEPY GUY: Pretty sure of yourself, aren't you?

GIRL: I'm very sure of myself.

(*Imitating John Wayne from* The Spoilers, *1947.*)

"Now I think it's time we understood each other a little better. Come here."

(CREEPY GUY *approaches.*)

"From here on, things are gonna be run my way. And you can start adjusting to it."

(*She kisses him, he resists, then eases into it. She breaks the kiss.*)

"And that's my way. Like it?"

(*She twirls the gun and puts it in her belt.*)

And that's how it is. Everybody's somebody.

(*Then she walks out the door to the accompaniment of the theme from* The Good, the Bad, and the Ugly.)

The End

Feet

Aden Ross (1944–) has published plays, poetry, short stories, literary criticism, and reviews. *Rings,* a runner-up in the Humana Festival at the Actors' Theatre of Louisville and in the Rosenthal New Play Competition, was produced by Park City Performances and given a staged reading at the Utah Shakespearean Festival in 1993. Also in 1993, *F. F. the Brontes* was commissioned and produced by the Salt Lake Acting Company, which had previously produced Ross's *K-Mille, Shroud Lines,* and *Wanted: Billy the Kid. Oedipus Unbound* was staged at the Sundance Playwrights' Lab and then opened at the Actors' Theatre in Baton Rouge. Ross just completed *Dreamkeepers,* the libretto for the Utah Centennial Opera commissioned by the Utah Opera Company. She is currently writing a feminist western musical comedy, scheduled to open in 1995 in Salt Lake City. Ross earned her Ph.D. in English at the University of Utah, where she is an adjunct associate professor of theatre.

Feet played Off-Off-Broadway in 1987 and in
the 1990 *Utah Shorts* by Theatreworks West; it
often tours Utah with the Rural Arts
Consortium.

CHARACTERS

> The characters can be played by actors of any race or ethnicity.

Freddie

> *a young woman*

Lanny

> *a man about* FREDDIE*'s age*

TIME

Shortly after the Vietnam War

PLACE

An empty stage representing a back road in rural Utah

(On an empty stage, FREDDIE *and* LANNY. *She is holding a bundle representing a baby, and he is carrying a small broken child's tricycle. They are poor and are dressed accordingly:* FREDDIE *must be barefoot, and* LANNY *should be wearing a short-sleeved striped shirt and jeans.* LANNY *stands downstage of her. When* FREDDIE *is facing the audience, she is confiding her thoughts, and* LANNY *cannot hear her; some similar convention can be established when* LANNY *is voicing his memories without speaking in the present.)*

FREDDIE (*to the audience*): He just keeps walkin', Lanny do. Me 'n the baby been paddlin' after him some three miles. Where we goin', I'd like to know.

   (*Glancing at* LANNY.)

Don't dare ask. Whoo-o-o. Lanny say I talk too much.

   (*Pause.*)

It's mighty hot.

   (*To* LANNY.)

We're hot.

   (LANNY *briefly looks at her, then looks away. He jerks the tricycle or makes some similar angry gesture.*)

LANNY: Hot.

FREDDIE: Sweat's runnin' down Lanny's back like a little triangle cape. His shirt's that pretty stripe one I got on sale at Kmart. Only two ninety-nine. Wish I coulda got more. But Littlepop say, wishin' only hitches up the team. Wishin' don't plow.

   (*To* LANNY, *loud.*)

Wishin' don't plow.

LANNY (*stiffening, looking back at her*): Talk, talk, talk.

FREDDIE (*to* LANNY): That's what Littlepop say.

LANNY: Your pop's always got somethin' to say.

   (*Pause.*)

FREDDIE (*to the audience*): Lanny's got no daddy. His daddy left him. What would that be like?

   (*Cuddling the bundle in her arms.*)

Lanny is Sissy's daddy. Whoo-o-o, I'll never forget when I told him Sissy's his baby. . . .

FREDDIE (*overlapping with* LANNY): He so mad—	LANNY (*to the audience, in the past*): Not me, woman. No way.

FREDDIE (*to the audience*): What'd Lanny think? That I'd take up

with the likes of Buddy Smith or Cutter Johnson after I been
with him? He kept sayin' . . .

| FREDDIE (*overlapping with* | LANNY (*in the past*): Go on, get. |
| LANNY): Not me, get out— | GET. GET AWAY. |

FREDDIE: But once your feet set down, you stay.

(*Watching* LANNY.)

Whoo-o-o, he's yankin' Sissy's tricycle around. Been kickin' it in
the ditch, pullin' it out, kick again. What'd he bring that for. I
never seen Lanny so mad as today when I bring that trike home.
Bought it at the church rummage sale in the Safeway parkin' lot.

LANNY (*to the audience, in the recent past*): You what? You bought
that trash for your brand-new baby?!

FREDDIE (*to* LANNY, *in the past*): *Our* baby. She's your baby, too.

(*To the audience.*)

Did I hold my breath. He was screamin' to split a stump.

LANNY (*to the audience, in the past*): You're crazy. She's *not mine.*

FREDDIE (*to the audience*): Then he grabbed Sissy mean.

(*To* LANNY, *in the past.*)

You wanna slap somebody round, you slap *me* round. I won't
slap back. But you leave Sissy *be.*

(*To the audience.*)

He threw Sissy on Muz's couch and like to kick tricycle through
the screen door. Slammed that door behind him. Whoo-oo-eee.
I still be whipped, big as I am, if Muz hears me slam the screen.
Every time I slam the door, she yells at me, "You raised in a
barn? Or a chicken coop?" That sets me to giggle. Every time. I
giggle like Muz, even though she's not my mom. No sound
comes out, just belly jiggle. And Lord knows I got belly.

(*Pause.*)

Sissy was squallin', but she's quiet now. We been walkin' behind
Lanny the full length 'a Cottonwood Road. Must be headin' for
Deer Creek.

(*To* LANNY, *venturing.*)

We goin' to the creek?

(LANNY *does not respond. Pause.*)

(*To* LANNY, *to make conversation.*)

Ain't it hot, though?

LANNY (*jerking the tricycle*): Trash. Just trash. Got no money, and
you buy trash.

FREDDIE (*to the audience*): Lanny's shoulders ain't swingin' today.

His feet don't flitter like usual. First thing I ever seen on Lanny was his walk: Lanny's feet don't stay on the ground, don't belong. He don't have rodeo feet, exactly—not like Cutter Johnson. It's like balloons are liftin' Lanny so's all he can do is touch down barely. Best not tell him about the balloon I bought next door to the rummage sale. Seemed to me: a tricycle for Sissy and a balloon for Lanny. Just fits.

LANNY (*at her apparent silence, yanking the tricycle*): What you thinkin' now?

FREDDIE (*to the audience*): I remember the night I met Lanny. Whoo-oo.

(*To* LANNY.)

Remember, Lanny? The dance?

LANNY: Dance.

FREDDIE (*to the audience*): It was Saturday night at choir practice. We was in between the "Li'l Brown Church in the Wildwood" and the "Old Rugged Cross," when that jukin' music slips in the windows from the town hall. My feet sets to rappin'. Big Sis— she's a alto—elbowed me good. She whispered, "Set them feet still. You go jukin', I'll tan your hide. If Littlepop don't get you first." My feet kept rappin'. Sometimes feet do it all by their lonesome.

LANNY: What dance?

FREDDIE (*to the audience*): That night was so hot and dry, it felt like sandpaper. Mel's Drugstore stayed open late for ice cream. Ever notice streetlights make little star shapes if you squint up your eyes? It was that kinda night. I was wearin' my flare cotton skirt, not the gathered one. Makes a full pink circle, like a open flower. Sticks to my legs in the heat, though. Next thing I know, my feet is inside the town hall. And in come Lanny.

LANNY: What dance?

FREDDIE (*to* LANNY): When we met.

LANNY: Met? What you thinkin' now?

FREDDIE (*to the audience*): His eyes stayed on the ceiling. He do that a lot, like he's lookin' for a place to fly out the roof. Like the balloons will carry him off. His eyes dropped once to Rita Martinez.

(*Pause. To* LANNY.)

Remember Rita Martinez?

LANNY: Rita who?

FREDDIE (*reconsidering the moment*): What'd you expect, lookin' at Rita Martinez like that?

LANNY: Like what?

FREDDIE (*to the audience*): His eyes flicked right back up, though. Lanny don't look at folks much, neither. Hands stuffed in his pockets, tight jeans. Whoo-oo-eee. Jeans had paint flicks or somethin' white been washed in, but clean. There was Cutter in his rodeo belt and purple satin shirt. I calls out to Cutter, "What you think, wearin' that shirt?" He calls back, "Sexy." Well I thinks: cheap. Buddy Smith had just asked me to juke, but I seen Lanny. When I seen Lanny, my feet turned plum to cee-ment.

LANNY: What Rita look?

FREDDIE (*to* LANNY): Sissy's tired. I'm tired. I'd like to know how I'm gonna carry her to the creek, me walkin' barefoot.

LANNY: That's another thing: you barefoot.

FREDDIE (*to the audience*): Lanny's back don't show signs of slowdown. We're in big trouble.

| FREDDIE (*overlapping with* LANNY): When you're tired, Lanny say, the army say you do double time. | LANNY (*remembering*): . . . You're tired . . . the army say . . . do double time. |

FREDDIE: When you tired, I say stop.
    (*Pause.*)

FREDDIE (*to the audience*): Shows I'm too dumb to be in the army. Not Lanny, though. He fought in Vietnam. Lanny won't *never* talk about that. . . .

| FREDDIE (*overlapping*): Yap, yap, he say . . . Why I be askin' all the time about the war. | LANNY (*to the audience, in the past*): Talk, talk . . . Why you be asking all the time about the war. |

FREDDIE: Lanny once got so mad, got tears. Imagine: Lanny Brown cryin'. Lookin' and lookin' for a hole in the sky. Lookin' for a way out. Lanny was crying. . . .

| FREDDIE (*overlapping*): So many chilren . . . | LANNY (*in the past*): So many chilren . . . so *many*. Which is worse? The babies who get blowed up? Or all the babies left behind? All |

those babies without
daddies . . .

FREDDIE (*to the audience*): Lanny don't talk much, but when he do, his words send chills like faraway train whistles. You know, that choo-oo sound?

(*Faraway, wistful.*)

Choo-oo. From Muz's shack where we live, you can hear the train comin' down the canyon every mornin'. Your body be sound asleep, and your ears hear the train. Train tells your feet get up, go to work. Choo-oo, feet. That's what Lanny's words do. But nobody knows what he thinks. Littlepop always say, talk's cheap: watch their feet.

(LANNY *kicks the tricycle.*)

Ohoh. There goes the feet. There goes the tricycle.

LANNY (*turning toward her for the first time but avoiding her eyes*): So you say stop, huh?

FREDDIE (*to the audience*): That Saturday night dance, my feet turned plum to cee-ment. And stayed. With Lanny, I'm one of them toy tubes you turn, and the colors swap around: his hand goes click, and a new flower show. Maybe not a click. More like when the rain plops in the sand in front of Muz's shack.

(*Pause.*)

Muz is as good to me as a mom. Hope I be as good a mom as her. Funny how families are.

(*To* LANNY.)

Ain't it funny how families are?

LANNY: Families are what?

FREDDIE: Like Littlepop and Muz and Big Sis.

(*Pause, carefully.*)

You . . . and me . . . and Sissy.

LANNY: Why's Sissy fussin'?

FREDDIE: Why you think?

LANNY: She needs changin'.

FREDDIE: The sun'll rise tomorrow, too.

LANNY: Course, you don't bring nothin' for the baby.

(*Pause.*)

And lookit yer feet. Dammit, woman.

FREDDIE (*looking at them*): What's wrong with my feet?

LANNY: You got shoes. Where are they?

FREDDIE: I didn't have time to put 'em on, runnin' after you.

LANNY: What kinda trash run around barefoot?

FREDDIE: Littlepop say, feet goin' where they supposed to don't need shoes.

LANNY: Littlepop say, Littlepop say. You ever hear what I say?

(*Pause.*)

I say, you're a momma now. You ain't actin' like a momma.

FREDDIE: What about daddies?

LANNY: What about 'em?

FREDDIE: You ain't actin' like a daddy.

LANNY: How they act? I ain't had one.

FREDDIE: You *are* one.

(*Long, anguished pause.*)

LANNY: I . . . I *can't*. I *can't* be.

FREDDIE: Who you think I am, Lanny? You think I'd take up with Buddy Smith or Cutter Johnson after I been with *you?*

(*Long pause.*)

Lanny, we be all right.

LANNY: Yeah? How?

FREDDIE (*unconsciously handing the baby to* LANNY): We got . . .

LANNY (*starting to laugh, horribly*): We got what?

FREDDIE (*to the audience*): Ohoh. Lanny sometimes laugh sad and he sometimes laugh mean. We all in trouble when Lanny laugh mean.

(*To* LANNY.)

We got . . .

(*Retrieving the tricycle.*)

LANNY: No money. No job. No place.

(*Looking directly at her for the first time.*)

We got nothin'.

FREDDIE: Oh, when your eyes drop slam-bang from the sky to me, my heart likes to pop. Whoo-ee, man.

(*Pause.*)

LANNY: We got *tricycle*. That's what.

(FREDDIE *starts to giggle.*)

LANNY (*fighting it, but nonetheless slowly smiling at* FREDDIE's *infectious giggle*): How can you laugh?

FREDDIE: That's right. We got . . .

(*Looking at* LANNY *holding the baby.*)

Tricycle.

> (*Pause. Then, tenderly looking at her man and her baby, she can venture.*)

And at home . . . a balloon.

The End

This Is Dead Level

Red Shuttleworth (1944–) has had plays produced widely, including *Heart 'n Saddle Saloon* at the Churchill Arts Council in Fallon, Nevada. Red has also had readings of *62 Homers* at the Utah Shakespearean Festival, and *Wallet Mermaid* and *Pistolero Rideaway* at the Sundance Playwrights' Lab. He has published poetry, fiction, and drama in numerous journals. In 1989 Red received a Nevada State Council on the Arts Playwriting Fellowship. He earned his M.F.A. in playwriting from the University of Nevada, Las Vegas. Red is an assistant baseball coach and English instructor at Big Bend Community College in Moses Lake, Washington. *This is Dead Level* was first produced by State University of New York, College at Fredonia on March 6, 1995. Thomas W. Loughlin was producing director, and Peter Dimas served as director with the following cast: Christopher Thompson as "Alvin Blackhorse," Mary Regan as "Thora Green," Matt Osterhaus as "Eldon Lett," and Lauren Vollette as "Wendy Fenton."

Photo by J. A. Messicci

This Is Dead Level was first presented in a
reading at the University of Nevada, Las
Vegas, featuring the following actors: Charles
Paddock, Amy Shoopman, Davey
Marlin-Jones, and Lara Lanae Freeborn.

Alvin Blackhorse
forty-four

Thora Green
thirty-seven

Eldon Lett
sixty-five

Wendy Fenton
thirty-five

TIME
The present

PLACE
A room in the Copper Queen Casino and Motel in Ely, Nevada

(*A motel room at the Copper Queen.* ALVIN BLACKHORSE *is lying on his back, crossways, on the bed, his head on* THORA GREEN*'s lap.* ALVIN *is wearing his Jockey shorts.* THORA *is sitting on the bed, with her feet on the floor. She's in panties and a bra.*)

THORA: A silver ring's always kinda nice.

ALVIN: Ya think so?

THORA: Sure. I liked 'em when I was her age.

ALVIN: They're cheap, ain't they?

THORA: Yeah. So you wouldn't have to put out so much.

ALVIN: But I wanna get her somethin' to make up for all this time.

THORA (*pauses*): It's been nice, sugar, but I gotta go now.

ALVIN: Ya think I could get her a nice silver ring?

THORA: Absolutely.

    (*Pause.*)

Come on, raise up yer head.

ALVIN (*lifts his head, moves over*): You could help pick it out.

THORA (*stands*): I wish I could.

    (*Starts to get her skirt and blouse.*)

But good luck.

ALVIN: How long ya been doin' this?

THORA (*dressing*): There's a nice jewelry store downtown. You could check it out.

ALVIN: Ya never even said your name.

THORA: I work under the name 'a Dawn.

ALVIN: Okay.

    (*Pause.*)

How much for an afternoon?

THORA: To help you pick a ring?

ALVIN: Yeah.

THORA: Naw. I don't do that.

ALVIN: Another hun'red?

THORA: You got that much?

ALVIN: A bit more 'n that, yeah.

THORA: I make it a rule never to do anything real personal. Professional standards 'n all.

ALVIN: You might consider it like branchin' out, Dawn.

THORA: Sorry.

ALVIN: Then how about another fuck? Straight hun'red?

THORA: You ready again?

ALVIN: Could be.

THORA: I'll have to call in first.

ALVIN: Call in.

THORA: You sure? Like I know you must be short 'a money 'n all.

ALVIN: I like your style.

THORA (*pauses*): Money first.

ALVIN (*finds his wallet in his jeans*): This buys an hour, right?

THORA: If you can go that long, sugar.

> (*Pause.*)

Yeah, an hour. I didn't mean that as an insult or anything.

ALVIN: That's okay. What I mean is I got a car, 'n we can take the second half hour to go to that jewelry store.

THORA: You don't have no car. And if ya did, it's against rules for me to get into a car with you.

ALVIN: You could drive us. Ya allowed to pick up hitchhikers? I could hitch a ride, then you wouldn't be in a car with a customer.

> (*Holds out five twenty-dollar bills.*)
>
> (THORA *takes the money, sticks it in her purse.*)

THORA: You wanna do it in front 'a the mirror this time?

> (*She takes off her blouse, tosses it onto a chair.*)
>
> (ALVIN *goes to her, undoes her skirt, which falls to the floor.*)

ALVIN: Guess the first time was too ordinary, huh? Just that I been hemmed in for a couple years and needed it quick.

THORA: We can do it just an itty-bitty more ruffianistic. Or showy.

> (*A knock on the door.*)

ALVIN: That someone for you?

THORA: No. But I better call in.

ALVIN: I don't know anybody in Ely.

THORA: Maybe it's the maid or somethin'.

> (*More knocking on the door.*)

You get the door, 'n I'll call in. Then I'll do ya.

> (ALVIN *goes to the door and opens it.*)

ALVIN (*to* ELDON LETT, *who is still offstage*): What the fuck ya want?

ELDON (*offstage still*): Thora still here?

ALVIN: Go away, old man.   THORA: I'm here, Eldon. Let
                                      him in, okay?

> (ALVIN *lets in* ELDON, *who is in a rumpled old suit.*)

ELDON (*to* ALVIN): Got yer Sunday best on, huh?

> (*To* THORA.)

Thora, ol' Spunky is a dyin'.

ALVIN: Who is this guy?   ELDON: They think it's a stroke.

THORA: Oh, Eldon, I'm sorry!

(THORA *holds* ELDON.)

ELDON: He's gettin' summoned by the Lord.

ALVIN: I kinda like to be seduced right now, but the mood here is bummin' me out.

THORA (*to* ALVIN): I'm sorry. This is my stepdad. I'll give back your money.

ALVIN: I don't want my money back.

ELDON: I can wait outside. Ain't you done it yet? Yer boss says ya been here awhile.

THORA: Eldon, can you wait in my car? I'll give you the keys, okay?

ELDON: Spunky'll be dead by then.

ALVIN: Who the hell is Spunky?

THORA: His wife. Look . . . Mister . . .

ALVIN: Alvin.

THORA: Alvin, I ain't ever done this before to a customer, but I'm gonna give you your money back.

(*She retrieves her blouse.*)

ALVIN: Hold on. He said this person is a *he.* One 'a you is lyin' to me.

ELDON: Spunky's my dog. He's part Lab. Twelve years old. Thora lied so's we can just get outta this place. You can understand that, can't ya? Anyways, yer supposed to be a lot quicker at this.

THORA: He's close to that dog. It's all he's got.

ALVIN: Yeah. But right now, lady, you're all *I've* got. Plus I paid up.

(*Knock on the door.*)

Damn, who you got after you this time, lady?

ELDON: I tol' Shirley I was comin' to get you.

THORA: Shirley's his girlfriend. They hang out at the Seniors' Center.

(ALVIN *goes to the door, opens it, and a giant bunny rabbit walks in holding a tray of breakfast food and an envelope.*)

WENDY (*dressed as a bunny rabbit*): Alvin Blackhorse?

ALVIN: That's me.

WENDY: Today is your lucky day!

ALVIN: No, it ain't.

THORA (*steering* ELDON *toward the door*): Bye. I'll come back in an hour, okay?

ALVIN (*blocking* THORA *and* ELDON *from leaving*): Lemme jaw with you a bit over this!

WENDY: Alvin Blackhorse, your Easter Egg is the Winner!

ALVIN: What Easter egg?

WENDY: The first annual Easter Egg Draw for Cash 'n Prizes.

ELDON (*to* THORA): Thora, can you spot me ten bucks for some tangle-leg?

ALVIN: I'll take the cash. You keep the prize if it ain't gonna become cash.

WENDY: First you gotta get back into bed for the breakfast.

(ALVIN *drags* THORA *to the bed, forces her down on it.*)

ALVIN: Give the breakfast to Mrs. Blackhorse here.

ELDON (*to* THORA): You married him?

THORA: Eldon, sit down a minute, will ya?

WENDY (*serving* THORA *the breakfast tray*): But I have to present the envelope.

(*Takes the envelope, then to* ALVIN.)

On behalf of the Copper Queen Casino and Motel . . . the Grand Prize!

(WENDY *faints.*)

ELDON: She's had a stroke!

ALVIN (*pulling the rabbit head off* WENDY): Lady, hey, lady!

(*To* THORA.)

She's pourin' sweat.

THORA (*picks up a piece of sausage*): God, I ain't had nothin' to eat all day.

(ALVIN *unzips the rabbit costume, strips it off* WENDY, *then begins taking off her waitress outfit, too.*)

ELDON: Thora, I told the vet I'd be right back. He'll work on Spunky for charity, but I need that whiskey. Gimme the toast, okay.

(THORA *hands him the toast.*)

Vet thinks it was a stroke. With brain surgery there ain't no margins for errors.

(ALVIN *drags the half-awake* WENDY *onto the bed.*)

THORA: Alvin, open her envelope. See what you won.

WENDY: Geez, I feel bad.

THORA (*an arm around* WENDY'*s shoulders now*): Alvin, get a cool, damp washcloth, will ya?

ELDON (*picks up the envelope as* ALVIN *goes for the washcloth*): Hot damn, maybe the day's not all lost. I get a cut 'a this for bringin' him luck?

ALVIN (*back with a washcloth, which he hands to* THORA): Old man, gimme that envelope.

(*Receives the envelope and opens it.*)

WENDY: That you, Thora?

THORA: Yeah, Wendy, it's me.

WENDY: This is so embarrassing.

THORA (*wiping her brow*): Feel like some 'a this orange juice? You done sweat out a whole lake.

(WENDY *sips the orange juice.*)

ALVIN (*to* THORA): What's two hundred fifty pulls on the Quartermania worth?

THORA: When you gotta use 'em?

ALVIN: Today, by checkout time. Noon.

WENDY: I'd feel better if I was back to whorin'. I ain't gettin' back into that goddamned bunny suit again.

ELDON: I'll buy those two hundred fifty pulls at Quartermania from ya . . . for, say, thirty dollars.

ALVIN (*to* WENDY): They got a particular slot machine I gotta use?

WENDY: Yeah.   ELDON (*to* THORA): Thora, loan
                                 me thirty bucks.

ALVIN: Yer name's Thora, huh?

(*Pause.*)

Thora, let's go get that silver ring.

WENDY (*to* THORA): You married *him?*

THORA: He's got this thing 'bout wantin' me to help pick out some ring for his daughter.

ELDON: I'd venture you won't win squat on them machines. But I got the touch. How's about we go partners. That way I can pay the vet. I hate charity. This is dead level: I once whupped them machines for five grand in one day. Ask Thora. Happened when I was married to her late mother. They banned me from gamblin' for five years after. We go partners, you'll come out ahead.

WENDY (*to* ALVIN): Got a daughter? Really?

ALVIN: Over near Hawthorne. Yeah. Ain't seen her in a while.

WENDY: Thora, you ought to go with him.

(*To* ALVIN.)

How long they have you inside?

ALVIN: Seven years.

THORA: Had him about as long's you can keep an Indian on a bad rap.

(WENDY *picks up half a grapefruit.*)

WENDY: That's too bad, Alvin.

ALVIN: Yeah. But I did it.

THORA: You said you didn't.

ALVIN: No difference.

(*Pause.*)

Old man, you gotta go.

(ALVIN *takes out his wallet and hands* ELDON *a twenty-dollar bill.*)

ELDON: Thank you. I wouldn't 'a bothered you, but Spunky had the frothy mouth. Could 'a been rabies. But it was a stroke.

(*To* THORA.)

Can I take dinner at your place tonight?

THORA (*to* ALVIN): Really, I better go. Take your money back.

ALVIN: Only if you go to the jewelry store with me.

WENDY: Thora, you give me his money and I'll do the actual ramming bit.

THORA: Alvin, that okay? Wendy can get you back into the mood.

WENDY: I'm good as fired here anyway. And I'd do the jewelry store for you, too. What was you in for anyway?

ALVIN: You'll help me pick out a ring?

(THORA *and* ELDON *exit.*)

Hey, she left with the money!

WENDY: Relax. I know where to find her.

ALVIN: You want to shower first?

WENDY: After.

ALVIN: Okay.

(*He stands, doesn't move.*)

WENDY: Somethin' wrong?

ALVIN: Ya see . . .

WENDY: What? You want to do it with me in the rabbit getup? Toss it to me. With or without the rabbit's head?

ALVIN: What's your name?

WENDY: What it says on the name tag on my waitress costume: Wendy. Wendy Fenton. Married once. To a Darwin Silcox over in Wells. Hated the name. Hated the shuttered life. Also Darwin had a dinky little dick. You need to know anything else?

ALVIN: And what was her name?

WENDY: Thora Green. And that was Eldon Lett. They's married.

ALVIN: No.

WENDY: Okay, no. His dog have a stroke again? She punched her beeper alarm. You spooked her.

(ALVIN *picks up the rabbit outfit, half zips it back up, begins stuffing the bedspread into it, then the blanket.* WENDY *stands up, helps him stuff the outfit. They arrange the fully stuffed rabbit on the bed.*)

ALVIN: I'll get over it.

WENDY: That's for sure. Thora's okay 'n all, but nothin' special. We worked the same brothel for a time. You'll get over it.

ALVIN: I don't mean that. I mean asking names.

(*They force a pillow into the rabbit head, then set it atop the stuffed rabbit torso.*)

Names are just some kinda fanfare. Kinds of tattooed-on things. It's what you do . . . what you whisper at night. You understand?

WENDY (*puts the envelope and the prize certificate on the rabbit's torso*): Today is your lucky day, Alvin Blackhorse.

ALVIN: We'll be dream chasers.

(*They remove their remaining clothes.* ALVIN *picks up his wallet, empties it on the rabbit, flings away the wallet. With her arm around him, they exit.*)

The End

D-Day

Paavo Hall (1945–) was born in Bamberg, Germany, and came to America with his parents when he was four years old. Before attending high school in Las Vegas, he lived in California, Japan, and Washington. After completing his B.A. at the University of Nevada, Las Vegas, he served in Vietnam with the U.S. Army. Subsequently he earned his M.A. at the University of Nevada, Las Vegas, in history and an M.F.A. from the Yale School of Drama. While Hall was at Yale, his play about Hitler was produced, his *Aton* premiered at Yale Repertory Theater Sunday Series, and *Lester Leaps Out* opened at the Yale Cabaret. In 1979 he began teaching English at Mosul University in Iraq and was fired after writing a letter to Saddam Hussein requesting wartime tax relief during the Iran-Iraq War. Kozo Theater Development Corp. produced Hall's *The Thirty-six Dramatic Situations* (based on a work by the same title by Georg Polti); directed by James Simpson, the play opened at Rhode Island School of Design in 1982, then moved to Off-Off-Broadway. From 1985 through 1991, he taught at King Saud University in Saudi Arabia. Hall lives and writes plays in Las Vegas.

Photo by Sharron Mashburn

Joe

Phil

Ed

Diane

June 6, 1992

Las Vegas

(JOE *and* PHIL *are sitting in the fenced-in pool area of a Las Vegas apartment complex drinking beer. It is late in the afternoon.*)

JOE: Today is the forty-eighth anniversary of the greatest amphibious landing in the history of warfare. And that was only a part of the greatest, most colossal struggle in the history of mankind. Conservatively speaking, I'd say there were seventy million men in uniform on all sides when you include the war in Asia. Phil, how do you see my chances of being the last surviving veteran of World War II?

PHIL: Here in Vegas?

JOE: It was a world war, so I want to be the last one in the world.

PHIL: Your chances are better than they were last year.

JOE: Seventy million men started, and when the music finally stops, only one will be left to sit down, the last survivor.

PHIL: It'll probably be a Russian from that place where all they eat is yogurt.

JOE: Diet's important, but what really keeps a man going is desire. Take me. I still have a craving to be around beautiful young women. I figure as long as I have that, I'll be on my feet when the others drop.

PHIL: You know, they landed as many men in the Persian Gulf in a tenth of the time that it took them to get ready for D-day.

JOE: Yeah, but the Iraqis weren't the Germans. No air force, no navy, no brains. The days are over when equals meet on the battlefield.

PHIL: You don't think the Chinese were a match for us? You weren't there when they pushed us halfway across Korea.

JOE: And you weren't there when those German tanks busted through our lines at Bastogne.

PHIL: I heard about it, but everyone knew we had the Krauts outnumbered five to one. What people don't know is that the Chinese the night they crossed that river had us outnumbered ten to one. How do you like those odds?

JOE: I guess we've both been lucky.

PHIL: Luck? Hey, wait just a minute. I've got some medals to prove you wrong.

JOE: Maybe you were a brave son of a gun, but in my war the really brave ones didn't make it back. Maybe you were smart enough not to push your luck too far. There's nothing wrong with that. Now here comes a man who's lucky and doesn't even know it.

(*He is referring to* ED, *who is just entering the pool area.* ED *is in his early forties.*)

PHIL: Ah, that wasn't a war.

ED: What is it? Fifty years ago today that they let you crawl off that beach so you could live to have a few more beers?

JOE: Forty-eight to the day. Like I was telling Phil, I'm lucky to be alive. Here I am, seventy years old and healthy enough to drink both you youngsters under the table. I'd like to make a toast. Take a beer, Ed.

(ED *takes a beer and snaps it open.*)

To the prettiest lady of them all, to Lady Luck!

(*They drink.*)

PHIL: She's done all right by me. You know, the night the Chinese crossed the Yalu, my company lost half of its men before the sun came up.

JOE: Ten minutes after we hit Omaha Beach, every officer and two thirds of the NCOs in my company were dead. The rest of us just lay there on the open beach. In front of us every other step of ground had been mined. Even the sand crabs had been booby-trapped.

PHIL: Have any close calls in Nam, Ed?

ED: Sure did. Me and three buddies went on R and R to Bangkok. I was the only one who didn't come back with the clap.

JOE: You really don't appreciate how lucky you are to be alive.

ED: Hey, don't you believe it. Here I am in the middle of the ice age wearing a bathing suit. According to the geology books, we could be ice-skating tomorrow afternoon.

PHIL: Did you use a lot of drugs over there?

ED: I would describe my use of drugs as symbiotic. I used them, and they used me.

(*They see a very attractive young lady.*)

JOE: Is she yours?

ED: I borrowed her for the afternoon. Diane, I want you to meet Joe. He fought alongside Washington at the Chicken Ranch. And this is Phil, a veteran of the Battle of Tiajuana.

JOE: I'd be honored if you had a beer with us.

DIANE: No, thanks. I just couldn't. One more ounce and I'll bust out of this suit.

JOE: Live dangerously, Diane. This day was named after you. It's D-day.

DIANE: If I do some laps afterward, I suppose just one wouldn't hurt.

(JOE *opens a beer for her.*)

JOE: Let's drink to Lady Luck, who got me through the most colossal struggle ever fought by the human race.

(*They all drink.*)

ED: Your troubles aren't over yet, friend. I can see the day when wolves wander the icy streets, and I'll be skiing to Arizona.

DIANE: Oh, cut out that ice age crap, Eddie.

ED: Anyone who can't kill his food with his own bare hands will be a victim. Among those will be thousands of old war veterans who will be consumed as food and fuel by the young survivors.

JOE: If there's another ice age, I'll be around to shove your young bones down a hungry bear's throat.

DIANE: I didn't come for another argument. I'm going for a swim.

JOE: Diane, this is D-day. I guess in some ways I was lucky to survive, and in some ways, I wasn't. If I'd made a lot of money, I'd have a girlfriend your age right now sitting beside me.

PHIL: You still have some of that beach sand in your head, Joe.

JOE: I didn't know it then, but now I know it's true. Those men who died over there were carried off the battlefield in the arms of beautiful women. Diane, before you step into the water, would you let me kiss you?

DIANE: Is it all right, Eddie?

ED: Go ahead. Make the old lizard's day.

DIANE: That wasn't a very nice thing to say. My granddad was in that war too.

ED: Everyone's granddad fought in that one. There's millions of the fossils still around.

JOE: Is your grandfather still alive?

DIANE: I just got a call last week. They say he only has a few months left. Happy D-day, Joe.

(*They kiss.*)

JOE: Thank you, Diane.

DIANE: That was nice, Joe.

(DIANE *goes to the pool.*)

Eddie, this water's cold. Let's go inside.

ED: What I tell you guys. You can never tell when it's going to heat up or cool down.

(DIANE *and* ED *exit.* PHIL *goes to the pool.*)

PHIL: That water feels pretty warm to me.

JOE: It sure does. Phil, I think I'm going to make it. It's times like this that I just know I'm going to make it. I'm going to be the last survivor of the greatest war in mankind's history.

The End

BOB MAYBERRY

The Catechism of Patty Reed

Bob Mayberry (1950–) was born in San Francisco, California. He received his B.A. from the University of Nevada, Reno, in 1971, an M.A. from the University of Utah in 1974, a Ph.D. from the University of Rhode Island in 1979, and finished up with an M.F.A. in playwriting at the University of Iowa in 1985. Mayberry has written and cowritten eleven plays, with productions at the University of Rhode Island, the University of Iowa, the Street Players Theatre (Norman, Oklahoma), West Mesa High School (Albuquerque, New Mexico), the University of Nevada, Las Vegas, and the Rainbow Company Children's Theatre in Las Vegas. After teaching at the University of Nevada, Las Vegas, in the English department from 1985 through 1993, he joined the English department at the University of Alaska Southeast at Sitka.

The Catechism of Patty Reed was first produced
by the Rainbow Company Children's Theatre
in Las Vegas in May 1990.

Whether Patty Reed ever had this conversation with her mother or not, she was one of many children who survived the ordeal of the Donner Party in the Sierra Nevada the fall and winter of 1846–47. She raised a family of her own in San Jose and kept her precious doll with her until the day she died.

CHARACTERS

Patty
a girl of twelve or so

Margaret
her mother

James
her father

TIME
1846–47

PLACE
The Sierra Nevada

SET
Bare stage except for a straight-backed wooden chair

(PATTY *is seated on the chair holding a very worn and dirty rag doll. The doll is missing one of its arms. Her mother stands beside her.*)

MARGARET: Who is your father?

    (*No response. She snaps her fingers.*)

    Patty! Who's your father?

PATTY: James Reed.

MARGARET: James Reed of Illinois. Say it all.

PATTY: James Reed of Illinois.

MARGARET: Where is your father?

PATTY: Huh?

MARGARET: Pay attention, young lady. Where is your father?

PATTY: Uh, in California, I guess.

MARGARET: Don't guess. You're certain, aren't you? Aren't you?

PATTY: Yes.

MARGARET: Yes what?

PATTY: Yes, I'm certain.

MARGARET: You snap out of it right now, young lady. You hear me?
    Now put down that silly old doll and answer smartly. Who is
    your father?

PATTY (*still reluctant*): James Reed of Illinois.

MARGARET: Where is your father?

PATTY: California.

MARGARET: What was your father?

PATTY: What?

MARGARET: What was his job?

PATTY: Uh, leader?

    (MARGARET *indicates she expects more.*)

    Wagon-train leader.

MARGARET: Why is your father in California?

PATTY: How should I know?

MARGARET (*snapping fingers*): Why is he in California?

PATTY: (*sarcastic*): Trying to save us?

MARGARET: Don't give me any lip. What did your father promise
    you?

PATTY: To come back, but that was—

MARGARET: No buts, young lady. To come back, that's the answer,
    nothing more, understand? Again, what did your father promise?

PATTY (*repressing anger*): To come back.

MARGARET: When?

PATTY: As soon as he could.

MARGARET: Could what?

PATTY: As soon as he could.

MARGARET: That's not all of it, Patty. As soon as he could what?
(*No response.*)
Say it, all of it, or we'll start over, young lady, until you get it right.

PATTY: Get over the mountains.

MARGARET: It's important, you know that, don't you? I wouldn't make you do this if it wasn't important. They're going to tell you lies when I'm gone. You must be ready with the answers. Fight their lies with the truth. You understand, Patty? You're a big girl now.

PATTY: But why'd he have to go?

MARGARET: Hush now. You know why. Do you believe your father?

PATTY (*unconvinced*): Yes.

MARGARET: Who made Daddy leave us? Huh?

PATTY: They did.

MARGARET: Who?

PATTY: Those men.

MARGARET: Mr. Keseberg?
(PATTY *nods affirmatively.*)
Mr. Breen?
(*She nods.*)
Mr. Donner?

PATTY: No, not Uncle George.

MARGARET: Good girl. Now, why did they make Daddy leave?

PATTY: Because he killed that man.

MARGARET: How?

PATTY: Uh, with a knife?

MARGARET: Sorry, dear, I meant . . . did Daddy do it on purpose, or was it an accident?

PATTY: Accident.

MARGARET: Good. Come here. Momma has to go very soon.

PATTY: No.

MARGARET: Hush, baby, hush. We're all going to be fine. You and Momma and Daddy. Where will we all be together again? Where?

PATTY: California.

MARGARET: California. What's it like in California?

PATTY: No snow.

MARGARET: That's right. No more snow. And what else?

PATTY: A farm for Momma and Daddy.

MARGARET: What else?

PATTY: A house.

MARGARET: What for Patty?

> (PATTY *crushes her doll to her.*)

What for Patty? Remember? Momma promised Patty . . . what? A new doll! Remember?

> (PATTY *responds by holding her doll closer to her.* MARGARET *reaches into a pocket and pulls out a small shred of meat.*)

MARGARET: I saved this for you.

> (*She places the meat in* PATTY's *hand as carefully as if it were a robin's egg.* PATTY *doesn't believe what she sees.*)

Save it. It's all there is. Until you have to. Don't tell anyone. You understand?

PATTY: But where? How? What—

> (MARGARET *puts a finger to* PATTY's *lips to silence her.*)

MARGARET: Our secret. Remember Billy?

PATTY: He ran away.

> (MARGARET *shakes her head.*)

But you said . . .

> (MARGARET *wraps her hands around* PATTY's *and the meat.*)

No!

MARGARET: We finished the oxen weeks ago, before the last snowfall. There's been nothing but hides to eat. You got so sick, remember?

PATTY: I don't remember that far.

MARGARET: I know. Seems like years. Four months, Patty. Four months, and there's nothing left. No flour, no oxen, not even any dogs. The Breens ate their hound two weeks ago. People are dying. You know that, you're a big girl. I can tell you that, can't I? You might have died too, Patty. Billy saved you.

PATTY: I . . . ate . . . my dog, my own dog?

MARGARET: And got well. And lived. I'll be back for you, Patty. I promise. Momma promises.

PATTY: Daddy promised.

MARGARET: He's tried, Patty. I know he's tried. I see him, in my dreams, trying to get back over the mountains to save us. That's why I'm going, to help him. To help Daddy come save us.

PATTY: I want to go.

MARGARET: Oh, baby, I wish . . . I can't carry you, you know that.

PATTY: I'll walk.

MARGARET: Remember the first time we tried? After the first snow. We'd only been here a short while. Everyone was so hopeful. We cut the boughs of the trees and made snowshoes, remember? And we almost made it to the top. Almost.

PATTY: I'm older now.

MARGARET: We're weaker now. We'd both starve up there. You stay here and stay alive. Don't tell anyone about this.

(Indicating the meat.)

Chew it slowly, one bite a day. I'll be back.

(MARGARET starts to walk off.)

PATTY: I'll starve.

MARGARET: The Breens will share with you.

PATTY: They hate me! I'd rather die with you.

MARGARET: Don't, Patty, for Momma, for Daddy, for all of us. I wouldn't want to live without you. Hush now. Everything will be all right. Shhh.

(MARGARET kisses her daughter's forehead and exits. PATTY sits in silence, holding her doll. She stares blankly at the audience as if expecting them to speak to her. After a moment, she takes a small bite of the meat and chews it slowly, deliberately. She swallows. Then she turns the doll so it too faces the audience, and she begins to question it, just as her mother questioned her. Her voice is remote, hopeless. But she grows more animated as her confidence in what she says grows.)

PATTY: Who is your father?

(Doll's voice.) James Reed.

That's not all of it.

James Reed of Illinois.

Who is your mother?

Margaret Reed.

Where is your father?

In California.

Where is your mother?

(Hesitant.) Climbing the mountain.

Why did your father leave you?

I don't know.

You do too!

To save us.

Why did your mother leave you?

(*Pause.*)

Say it!

To save us?

Are you saved? Huh? Are you? No! So you lied. You're a liar. Aren't you?

(*Shakes doll violently.*)

Aren't you?

(*Frightened.*)

Yes.

Can you tell the truth? Can you?

Yes.

So? Tell it.

Momma's mad at me.

Momma loves you.

I eat too much.

There's nothing but crumbs.

I stole some crumbs. Momma's crumbs. She was saving. I ate them, so now she has to leave me. She said she wouldn't want to live without you.

(*With this outburst, the doll's voice and* PATTY'*s become one.*)

THEN WHY DID SHE LEAVE? SHE'S GOING TO DIE NOW LIKE DADDY, AND THEN WE'LL NEVER BE TOGETHER IN CALIFORNIA, AND IT WILL ALL BE MY FAULT.

(*Silence.* PATTY *lets the doll fall limply into her lap or hang from one hand. She's ashamed. She can't look up for some time. Then she speaks to the audience.*)

I eat snow. Every day it's something different. I pretend. Snow biscuits. Snow milk. Snow potatoes. Snow soup. Even . . . even snow meat. (*In a rush.*) I didn't mean to eat my dog, Billy. I didn't know. I mean, I was hungry and didn't notice what I was eating, and I'll never . . . (*looking at the meat in her hand*) . . . ever . . . eat . . . meat—

(*She shoves the meat into her mouth and chews until she has swallowed it all. She licks her hand, then her lips.*)

I'm sorry, Billy. I'm sick of snow. Mr. Breen told his wife not to feed me. There wasn't enough for their children, he said. I watched them eat it every night. Mrs. Breen took a spoonful of gray stuff out of the pot—it smelled horrible—and fed the baby first. Then a spoonful for each of the children. One for Jimmy. One for Peter. And Simon and Patrick, Edward and . . . and the oldest boy—I don't know his name.

(*Counting them on her fingers.*)

Seven spoonfuls. I watched them eat. Every night. I tried to curl up in the doorway, but the wind came in under the flap. In the middle of the night, when Mr. Breen was snoring, Mrs. Breen let me sit in the corner with the baby.

(*Holding the doll close.*)

It kept me warm. She always saved a crumb of bread or piece of hide I could suck on. She told me to never tell Mr. Breen.

(*She looks the doll in the face as if making a decision.*)

We never told, did we? We've never told anybody. And we'll never tell, will we?

(*She holds the doll so it faces the audience and speaks in its voice.*)

It's our secret. Patty's and mine. We heard things, at night. Sounds. Coming from the other side of the wall.

(PATTY *puts her hands over the doll's mouth to stop herself from telling. She speaks to the doll as her mother spoke to her.*)

Hush, baby. Everything is all right. Momma and Daddy promised. Momma and Daddy always keep their promises. Don't they?

(*Frightened by the thought.*)

Everything was pretty. Pretty pretty white. I forgot about being hungry while I sat on my rock and listened to the ice cracking in the lake and watched the blackbirds fly from tree to tree and watched for Momma and Daddy to come down from the top of the white mountain and save me. I imagined them like angels, dressed all in white, floating down out of the blue sky and carrying me off into the clouds where everything was pretty pretty white . . . pretty pretty . . . white.

(PATTY *seems to fade out, probably from hunger. Pause. Then the doll speaks.* PATTY *responds as if in a dream.*)

Patty? Patty, did you die?

Yes, I died. And went to heaven.

What was heaven like?

White. Everything was white.

Was anybody there?

Momma and Billy and Grandma and . . . Everyone was there.

Even Keseberg?

No!

Mr. Breen?

No. But Mrs. Breen was. Her baby was so pretty. All white.

Patty? Was Daddy there?

(PATTY *is too weak to answer. Silence, then* JAMES *enters upstage and crosses down to* PATTY.)

JAMES: Yes, Patty, Daddy was there. But it wasn't heaven. It was right here, remember? It took a long time, and Daddy almost died, but he kept his promise. He came back. He saved you. Remember?

PATTY: And Momma?

JAMES: Momma too.

(MARGARET *appears upstage and crosses wearily down to* PATTY.)

We both came back. And just in time. You were starving, baby. The food was all gone. Even the meat that Momma gave you.

MARGARET: Did you chew it, Patty? Chew it slowly?

JAMES: You were weak from hunger. But Daddy brought . . .

(*He reaches into his pocket and brings out crumbs. He is dismayed. They slip through his fingers. He hastily gathers them up.*)

MARGARET: Bread. Daddy brought bread.

(*She falls to her knees and stuffs crumbs into her mouth.* JAMES *saves some for* PATTY.)

JAMES: Bread.

(*He places some crumbs on* PATTY's *lips. She is too weak to chew. He helps her get started.*)

Do this. That's it. Slowly. Good girl.

(PATTY *revives some.*)

Feeling better?

PATTY: Where . . . how?

JAMES: How'd I get here? Over the mountains. You watched me. All morning you sat on your rock there and watched me hike around the lake to get to you. I waved. Why didn't you wave back?

(*Pause.*)

You said I looked like an angel descending from the clouds.

(*To* MARGARET.)

That's what she said. Her father looked like an angel coming to save her.

PATTY: No, Daddy, you weren't the angel.

JAMES: Of course I'm not an angel. You were seeing things. The sunlight on the snow blinded you. What you saw was an apparition. Remember on the desert how we thought we saw water? Do you remember the word for those apparitions? Do you?

PATTY: Daddy wasn't the angel.

MARGARET: Of course not, dear. Angels live in heaven. You saw Daddy across the snow and he looked like an angel.

PATTY: I was in heaven. Everything was white.

MARGARET: Daddy gave you food and brought you back. You were almost lost to us, do you know that?

PATTY: I wish he'd left me there.

JAMES: She's delirious.

PATTY: I wasn't hungry.

MARGARET: She doesn't know what she's saying.

JAMES: She needs to rest.

MARGARET: It's a miracle she's alive.

JAMES: It was too much for her.

MARGARET (*reaches for the doll*): Look, Patty, your doll is missing its arm. Momma will get you a new one.

(PATTY *grabs the doll from her.*)

PATTY: He ate it!

JAMES: You're crazy from hunger, baby.

MARGARET: I'll get you a new one when we get to California.

PATTY: NO!

(*She jumps onto the chair and stands there protecting the doll.*)
YOU CAN'T HAVE HER. YOU LEFT HER BEHIND.
SHE'S NOT YOURS.

MARGARET: It's all right, Patty, everything's all right. I won't take it away.

JAMES: Your mother just thought a new one would, well, help you forget about all this.

PATTY: I'LL NEVER FORGET IT.

MARGARET: Hush now, baby. Shhh.

JAMES: Everything's going to be just fine.

(Throughout the following, PATTY *is squirming, as if something is trying to come out of her. She holds the doll away from her body, with both hands, and makes it squirm violently. She is half muttering, half crying, overlapping the others. Rapidly.)*

PATTY: No.

JAMES: I promise.

MARGARET: Yes, Patty.

JAMES: It's all over now.

MARGARET: Daddy promises.

PATTY: No.

JAMES: We'll be together in California.

MARGARET: And what's California like, Patty?

PATTY: No.

MARGARET: Tell your father. What's California like? You know the answer.

*(*PATTY *screams shrilly. Her squirming ceases abruptly, and she thrusts her doll over her head with both hands.)*

PATTY: Tell them.

(Shaking the doll.)

Tell them what you saw. Say it!

(The way she moves the doll and the timidity in her voice make it apparent the doll is speaking her secret.)

It was dark in there.

In where?

In the room where I saw him.

Who?

Mr. Breen.

What was he doing?

Eating.

What did you see?

(Pause.)

Say it.

An arm.

Whose arm? Whose arm?

MY ARM!

*(*PATTY *makes the doll dance above her head. Her voice and the doll's have merged again.)*

MY ARM! MY ARM!

MARGARET: What's she mean?

JAMES: She's confused. It's a nightmare. She's having delusions.

PATTY: It can't be your arm. Not your arm. You're a doll. Whose arm? WHOSE ARM, PATTY?

(PATTY *turns deliberately to face her mother. She cries out her accusations in her own voice.*)

THE BABY'S ARM, IT WAS THE BABY'S ARM, AND YOU MADE ME STAY WITH HIM, YOU LEFT ME, LEFT ME WITH HIM.

MARGARET: Who? What?

PATTY: MR. BREEN, IT WAS BABY BREEN'S ARM.

(*Silence, then quietly.*)

He was eating his baby.

(PATTY *collapses in the chair, clutching the doll.*)

JAMES (*quietly*): Oh. My. God.

MARGARET: She's making it up, she doesn't know what she's saying, it's a delusion, you said so yourself. I didn't know, I didn't know . . .

JAMES: You left her with . . .

MARGARET: I had no choice. We were starving.

JAMES: Better starvation than . . . that.

(*To* PATTY.)

I'm sorry, baby, I didn't know. Patty.

(*He reaches out to comfort her, but she slaps his hand away.*)

PATTY: You left us to starve. You made us move to California. You said it was pretty. You said life would be better. You said we'd have as much food as we could eat. YOU LIED.

JAMES: I came back like I said I would. I saved you.

PATTY: Better dead than this.

(*Silence.*)

JAMES: Patty, we're sorry.

MARGARET: We're sorry, baby. Forgive us.

(PATTY *looks at her doll as she decides, then hands it to her mother, gently, before turning her back to her parents and speaking to the audience. She struggles to make sense of what has happened.*)

PATTY: I ate Billy. Mr. Breen ate the baby. We lived. For a while. Then there was nothing but snow to eat. I died and angels came to take me to heaven. But Daddy fed me crumbs and . . . and now I'm alive.

(*Pause.*)

I can't hate them. He crossed the mountains. She saved the meat for me. But how can I forgive them? I'll never forget what the world looked like when I was a child. Never forget the taste of snow. Every night as I lay in bed I hear Mr. Breen in the next room, and I smell that smell. I fall asleep remembering.

(PATTY *turns and sees her parents, then exits upstage, alone.*)

The End

Dance Saturday Night

John D. Newsom (1953–) was born in Lubbock, Texas, and has lived in Las Vegas ever since he was eight years old, with the exception of the four years he served in the air force. He has a B.A. and M.A. in English from the University of Nevada, Las Vegas. His master's thesis was a novel, and he credits his dissatisfaction in that effort with prompting him to try his hand at drama. Newsom was the first person to gain an M.F.A. in playwriting at the University of Nevada, Las Vegas. His locus for his writing is routinely found in the Southwest. Newsom's thesis play, produced at the University of Nevada, Las Vegas, *A Walking Shadow,* is the last play to have been directed by Jerry L. Crawford. Newsom's playwriting influences include Horton Foote, Eugene O'Neill, Anton Chekhov, and Henrik Ibsen. Newsom has been an instructor in the University of Nevada, Las Vegas, freshman composition program for fourteen years.

Photo by Judy McClendon

Lyle
*about thirty, wearing ordinary working clothes for a cowboy—
but with dinner jacket and a string tie*

Hector
about thirty, wearing much the same clothes as Lyle

Alex
about twenty-five, wearing a reasonably inexpensive suit

Thelma
about thirty, wearing a somewhat daring party dress

TIME
1890; evening

PLACE
Street outside a community meeting hall in Prescott, Arizona

SET
The meeting hall features two heavy wooden doors, a covered veranda, various pieces of outdoor furniture, a railing that encloses the veranda except for the stairs that allow access to the street. Gas lamps are located at each end of the meeting hall and are lit.

(Ragtime music fades in. The music is sustained for a few bars and then stops. Applause can be heard from within the meeting hall. HECTOR *enters from the front doors of the hall. He takes a flask from his coat and drinks. He attempts to descend the stairs, briefly loses his balance, and nearly drops the flask. He steadies himself, then sits at the bottom of the steps. He drinks again, just as* LYLE *enters from the front doors.* LYLE *is less drunk than* HECTOR, *but not much less. He sits beside* HECTOR.)

LYLE: Let me have some of that.

HECTOR: Buy your own.

LYLE: Haven't got the money for it. Let me have some of yours.

HECTOR: So I'm buying for me *and* you? Since when I gotta support you?

LYLE: You got a bad memory, Hector. Man who can't remember as far back as yesterday needs to look out for himself.

(LYLE *snatches the flask away from* HECTOR *and drinks.*)

HECTOR: Gonna learn you about that, one of these days.

LYLE: This ain't store-bought.

HECTOR: Taking my whiskey outta my hand like that—gonna learn you.

LYLE: It's taking the skin right off my teeth. *Can't* be store-bought.

HECTOR: Either kill you or cure you. One of the two.

(HECTOR *takes the flask back and drinks.*)

LYLE: Where'd you get it, Hector?

HECTOR: Store-bought liquor's for widows and old maids.

LYLE: You see that nigger in there?

HECTOR: Temperance League can shut down ever' saloon in the country, for all I care.

LYLE: Never seen anybody dance like him. You?

HECTOR: There *oughta* be a law against saloons calling it whiskey, anyway. Closer to soda water.

LYLE: Never saw such high-stepping in my life.

(HECTOR *hands* LYLE *the flask. The exchange will occur regularly throughout the scene.*)

HECTOR: Saw all kinds of niggers dancing that way when I took my ride on a Mississippi steamboat.

LYLE: Didn't know a body could move that way.

HECTOR: Natural for them. They been dancing that way all along.

LYLE: You think so? They was born that way?

HECTOR: All they got in common with us is the clothes white men give them.

LYLE: They got that kinda music in Africa?

HECTOR: How do I know? Whatever music gets played, they're ready to dance to it. It's *in* them. Never seen a nigger who *can't* dance.

LYLE: Sure was a sight to me. Never imagined.

HECTOR: You can see that ever' night on the Mississippi. I swear.

LYLE: Sometime I'm just gonna find out for myself.

HECTOR: Dancing's the best thing for them.

LYLE: Where'd you get that idea?

HECTOR: Let them dance all they want. Nothing like tired nigger for being easy to get along with. No trouble out of him at all.

(ALEX *enters from the front doors. He steps down between* HECTOR *and* LYLE *and moves to exit.*)

LYLE: Hey, you done tonight?

ALEX: Looks like it.

LYLE: That sure was a sight in there.

ALEX: You mean my dancing.

LYLE: I *never* seen nobody strut and kick like that before.

ALEX: I do my best when I get the chance.

LYLE: Wouldn't be surprised if you was dog-tired after that.

ALEX: Have to pace yourself.

LYLE: Shame you're quitting so early.

ALEX: Didn't come to dance by myself.

HECTOR: Too bad there wasn't no girl for you in there.

ALEX: There ain't *that* kinda girl for a hundred miles in any direction.

HECTOR: Why in blazes you out here in Arizona, Leroy?

ALEX: The name's Alex.

LYLE: What brought you out here, though?

ALEX: Same thing that brings most folks out here.

HECTOR: What used to be home to you . . . Alex?

ALEX: Georgia.

HECTOR: That's a long way from the Arizona Territory.

ALEX: People around here keep telling me that.

LYLE: What was wrong with Georgia?

ALEX: If you'd ever been there, you wouldn't ask.

HECTOR: Just picked up and left? Came west on pure inclination?

ALEX: West is where you come when there ain't nothing worth nothing where you are.

LYLE: We got an idea. Me and Hector's been drifting west since we met up in Texas.

HECTOR: Got a trade, Leroy? Nobody's gonna pay you much for singing and dancing.

LYLE: Bet he could earn room and board with it down in Phoenix or Tucson.

ALEX: Singing and dancing ain't all my capability.

HECTOR: Ain't no cotton fields out here. No watermelon patches neither.

ALEX: I worked a couple cattle ranches from the Red River on.

LYLE: He been a *cowboy?*

HECTOR: A cowboy that dances the way you do?

ALEX: The steers like the singing better than the dancing.

(THELMA *enters from the front doors.*)

HECTOR: Ain't nobody who can dance that way and call himself a cowboy.

LYLE: Maybe it's because we never seen a cowboy as good at it as him.

HECTOR: Ain't natural for a cowboy.

LYLE: What the blazes does a cow know about what's natural?

THELMA: They're fixing to start up in there again.

HECTOR: A cow knows what *ain't* natural.

THELMA: That band ought to be right jolly this time. They been at the punch bowl ever since they stopped.

LYLE: Got your second wind, Thelma?

THELMA: My feet ain't sore, and my toes ain't got blisters.

LYLE: You and Alex was sure fine to watch in there.

THELMA: Alex is his name then?

ALEX: I answer to it.

THELMA: Mine's Thelma. Must say I never saw a man move like you do.

HECTOR: We been through that.

ALEX: You ain't so bad yourself . . . Thelma.

THELMA: Wasn't your idea to sit out here and let these boys poison you with their rat killer, was it?

ALEX: They didn't pass me any of it.

THELMA: Some of the firewater they swear by can blind you as soon as you pull the cork.

ALEX: Looks like they had a mind to protect my health.

LYLE: That ain't fair, Thelma. We wouldn't offer Alex nothing we wouldn't drink ourselves.

THELMA: That covers a lot of territory, Lyle.

LYLE: We *woulda* offered Alex some of our brew. Just hadn't got around to it.

(LYLE *hands the flask to* ALEX.)

You try that, Alex. I ain't saying it's the best whiskey I ever had—but it ain't done no serious damage to me nor Hector.

(ALEX *drinks. A pause.*)

ALEX: That's enough to make the dead sit up and wonder why.

LYLE: The old man that makes it says he's got a secret way of aging it.

HECTOR: Son of a bitch ages it with whatever he can trap. Mice, rats, possum . . . or coon.

THELMA: Give me some of it too.

(ALEX *hands her the flask, and* THELMA *drinks. A pause.*)

Set me on fire, boys. Might as well burn me *all* up.

(*The music resumes within the meeting hall.*)

Your brain too furry to recollect how your feet is supposed to move?

ALEX: My mama said I was dancing when she was carrying me. I *know* I'll be dancing at the Pearly Gates.

HECTOR: Make it a habit of drinking my whiskey, you'll find out sooner than later.

THELMA: Let's go in and show them what we got left in us.

LYLE: Why not show us out here?

THELMA: Out here? Just him and me?

LYLE: Ain't nobody in there can dance like you two. You're all there is to watch.

ALEX: Suits me.

(ALEX *and* THELMA *begin to dance. After a moment,* HECTOR *takes the flask from* LYLE.)

HECTOR: Gimme that.

(HECTOR *tries to drink, then realizes the flask is empty.*)

It's all gone.

LYLE: Went to a good cause.

HECTOR: I was gonna get drunk on this.

LYLE: Hell, you're already drunk.

HECTOR: Wasn't even yours to give away.

LYLE: Let's watch them dance, Hector. Ain't ever' day we get to watch something this good.

(*The dance continues, and an increasing sexuality is expressed between* ALEX *and* THELMA.)

HECTOR: Don't like this at all.

LYLE: We can get more. I got money.

HECTOR: What the hell you *giving* my liquor away for?

LYLE: I was being friendly.

HECTOR: Was it *your* goddamned whiskey?

LYLE: How much of my whiskey's passed between your teeth, Hector?

HECTOR: Never gave it to nobody else without asking.

LYLE: How many times I heard you give out please-and-thank-you's for my whiskey?

HECTOR: Never gave none of it to no strangers.

LYLE: Not when you were half-sober, you didn't.

HECTOR: *Never once gave it to no nigger in the woodpile, did I?*

(ALEX *and* THELMA *stop dancing.*)

Look at what he's trying to pull. Right here in front of us. Give him a free drink, and look at what he tries to pull.

LYLE: Can't see that he's pulling anything. He's a cowboy in town on a Saturday night.

HECTOR: *He ain't no cowboy.* That monkey-dancing just proves it.

THELMA: You better stick your head under the nearest pump, Hector. You're liable to get it kicked real quicklike.

HECTOR: By Leroy?

THELMA: Don't know about Alex here, but you're getting on *my* nerves.

LYLE: Keep that in mind, Hector. Remember what she did the last time she lost patience with you.

HECTOR: We ain't even seen him ride a horse.

LYLE: What we seen so far he does right well.

HECTOR: Let him tell us *one* outfit he's worked with.

LYLE: He ain't trying to get a job with *us.*

HECTOR: You stop to think of why he keeps on the move? Probably steals when everybody's gone from the bunkhouse. Bet you the sheriff's got paper on him.

THELMA: If he does, it's because Alex keeps running into ignorant chuckleheads like you.

HECTOR: I'm telling you this for your own —

THELMA: I been taking care of myself for a while now, Hector. Alex would have to be a rough customer to be worse than you on a bad night.

LYLE: Let's go back in, Hector. Maybe there's some of that punch left.

THELMA: You boys sure as hell don't need no more whiskey.

LYLE: Let's go in before it's all gone.

HECTOR: All them Sunday school teachers is crowded around it.

LYLE: Like ever' year. Let's see if any of the Temperance ladies have disgraced themselves.

HECTOR: Might as well get our money's worth outta that band.

LYLE: You got the right idea. I'm feeling like disturbing the peace tonight.

(LYLE *and* HECTOR *exit to the front doors.*)

THELMA: You coming in, Alex?

ALEX: Reckon not.

THELMA: Those Temperance ladies are a sight when they get pie-eyed.

ALEX: Lyle and Hector can pick up the slack.

THELMA: Hector takes some getting used to.

ALEX: He this way ever' time he gets drunk?

THELMA: He's a mean drunk — but he usually ain't dangerous.

ALEX: Only when he's looking in my direction.

THELMA: Hector's got a bad disposition — but it doesn't get worse unless he thinks you're afraid of him.

ALEX: I'm not.

THELMA: You know, I keep a place all to myself.

ALEX: You like your privacy.

THELMA: Everybody in Prescott knows who I keep company with is my business.

ALEX: Maybe some night you can hire a band and invite me to call.

THELMA: Maybe I don't have to hire the band.

ALEX: Knew a woman in Fort Worth who had a music box. Cheapest band you could get.

THELMA: You're not coming back in.

ALEX: Reckon not, Thelma.

THELMA: I keep a lantern in my front window. When it's burning, you can knock on my door.

ALEX: Everybody in this town know that?

THELMA: Everybody. I'm something of a scandal in Prescott.

(THELMA *kisses him.*)

ALEX: Go back inside. They're expecting you.

THELMA: I'll see you then?

ALEX: Along about payday. That suit you?

THELMA: It suits me.

(THELMA *exits to the front doors. After a moment,* ALEX *dances a few steps. He exits. Music is sustained for a few bars and then stops.*)

The End

From the Life of the Bog People

Brian Kral (1955–) has been a resident of Nevada and Arizona since 1960. In 1987 he became playwright-in-residence for the Rainbow Company Children's Theatre in Las Vegas, and in 1990 he was named artistic director, a position he maintained until 1993. He is the author of more than twenty plays, most of which are for young audiences. His plays have been published by Anchorage Press, in *West Coast Plays*, and in *Dramatics Magazine*. Kral has twice been the recipient of playwriting fellowships from the Nevada State Council on the Arts and has won a Governor's Arts Award for his contribution to Nevada's literature. Other honors include an Indianapolis–Purdue University (IUPUI) National Playwriting Award (1990), selection for the American Film Institute's professional television writers' workshop, and a Glendon Swarthout Award for fiction writing. Kral has a B.A. in theatre from the University of Nevada, Las Vegas, and an M.F.A. from Arizona State University. He is a member of the Dramatists Guild.

For Dorothy Webb

From the Life of the Bog People was first
performed on May 11, 1990, as part of the IF
Festival, a national symposium on
experimental or avant-garde plays for young
audiences, hosted by the Rainbow Company
Children's Theatre of the City of Las Vegas.

From the Life of the Bog People was written
under a Nevada State Council on the Arts
Playwriting Fellowship, funded, in part, by
the National Endowment for the Arts, a
federal agency.

The Man

The Boy

The Figure

The Voice

Early evening

One room in a small museum in Page, Arizona

A large display case lit by an overhead gallery spotlight. Two other display cases are also onstage: a tall, narrow case to the right and a square case to the left. These two cases—and their contents—are not illuminated. The first case is the widest and lowest of the three and is prominently in the center. Inside is a preserved FIGURE of a primitive man, his body painfully flattened, his flesh and clothing an identical monochrome color.

(Looking down at a large display case are a MAN *and a* BOY. *The exhibit in the case is concealed by their bodies. The* MAN *steps around behind the case, which contains the preserved* FIGURE.)

MAN: End of the line.

(Pause. He looks at an exhibit plaque.)

What's fascinating is that he's perfectly preserved.

*(*THE BOY *looks up, crosses around.)*

It says here that "in the unique process that occurred in the bog, this human figure was kept entirely intact." They think he might even have his last meal still sitting in his stomach.

BOY: Is that right?

MAN: Says so here.

BOY: They didn't dissect him?

MAN: No. "And no physical injury is in evidence."

BOY: So he's just the way he was when he sank in the swamp.

MAN *(nodding)*: Only uglier.

*(*THE BOY *studies* THE FIGURE.)*

And of course he's dead.

BOY: How come? If he's all together, and there's no physical injury?

MAN: What do you mean?

BOY: Why's he dead?

MAN: I don't know. Why don't you ask him?

BOY: I would, if I could.

(Pause.)

Where did he come from?

*(*THE MAN *looks at the exhibit plaque, but* THE BOY *continues to stare at* THE FIGURE *in the case.* THE FIGURE *lies on its side, facing the auditorium, arms and knees extended forward in something of a fetal position.)*

MAN: Doesn't say. I read that a lot of them were dug out of peat bogs in England and Denmark. But I guess they've found them buried in prehistoric swamps in Georgia and Florida too, and even up on the Canadian coast. . . . How old do you suppose he is?

(No response from THE BOY. THE MAN *nods.)*

Yeah, it's kind of hard to tell. From pictures I've seen, they all kind of look like those shriveled-up apple sculptures—

(He tries to approximate the expression.)

—even the young ones.

(He repeats the same face.)

BOY: If you look at just the right angle, . . . the light shines on his skin. You can see yourself reflected there.

(THE MAN *kneels down to* THE BOY's *eye level and studies* THE FIGURE *impassively. Pause.*)

MAN (*straightening up*): This is exactly what I like about the desert. Out here, everything's laid out in orderly layers of sand. History, with all the mess stripped away. Whether you're walking around an old cliff dwelling, or picking through the parts of a dried cow carcass, it's all as neat as a Navajo sandpainting. But *this* . . .

(*He shakes his head at the display case.*)

Well, this kind of thing could only happen to you in a wet climate.

BOY: How do you think he got *here?*

MAN: Truthfully?

(THE BOY *nods.*)

Somebody probably bought him. Like that Elephant Man.

(THE BOY *returns his attention to the case.*)

You ready to go?

BOY (*intent on* THE FIGURE): I'd like to stay a little longer.

MAN: I don't know what you find so fascinating. How can you stand there, looking at one thing like that? I couldn't do it.

BOY: He's interesting.

MAN: So you said. You must see something that I don't.

(*Pause.* THE MAN *walks to the tall, narrow case at the left, flips on a switch. An overhead spot illuminates the contents of the case: a primitive spear. Brief pause. Then he flips off the switch and the case goes black.*)

I'm glad we found something you like, though. It's your trip too, "after all."

(*He looks at his watch.*)

And it's just about over. They'll be locking those doors soon. Do you want to go see the dinosaur bones?

BOY (*intent on* THE FIGURE): I want to stay here a little bit longer.

(*Pause.*)

MAN: Sure.

(*He too looks at* THE FIGURE *in the case.*)

You know, your grandmother used to say that if you wanted to see the future, you just stare deep into a dead man's eyes. . . .

(*Menacingly.*)

Aren't you afraid of that?

BOY: Of what?

MAN: Seeing your future. Seeing how we'll end up.

   (*Pause.*)

BOY: Did she really say that?

MAN: Don't you remember?

BOY: I can't remember Grandma.

MAN: That's too bad. You would have liked her. People were smaller
   then. She was just a slip of a thing, a small sip of water. You
   could've put her in this case. Though I don't think she would've
   liked being in there with *him*.

   (*Pause.* THE BOY *steps around to the front of the case.* THE
   FIGURE*'s eyelids are fused shut, but the mouth is open.*)

BOY: You can't see his eyes.

MAN (*reminiscing*): A skiff among the schooners. So . . . slight. A
   sliver.

BOY: But he's got a mouth full of teeth.

   (THE MAN *leans over to study* THE FIGURE*'s face.*)

MAN (*shaking his head*): Spissitude.

BOY: You're just jealous.

MAN: Of what?

BOY: All those teeth.

MAN (*considering this*): I might be at that.

   (*He looks at* THE FIGURE *once more.*)

   What do you find so interesting?

BOY: That he's a complete human being.

   (*Pause.* THE BOY *is intent on* THE FIGURE.)

MAN: I guess I'm from the supermarket school of museum
   watching. You know: browsing up and down the aisles, picking
   out the objects you really want to see; you stay for a second, then
   keep on moving to the next row of goods. I don't care to stay in
   one spot too long. And people get nervous if you stand there
   staring at the frozen-food case.

   (*He walks to the tall case to the left, flips on the switch. The
   overhead spot illuminates the primitive spear. He looks at it for a
   brief moment, flips off the switch. The case goes black. Pause.*)

   I'll head down this way. You can catch up with me later.

   (THE MAN *exits.* THE BOY *slowly circles the case, then stops
   behind it. He rests the palms of his hands flat on its top, to stare
   down at* THE FIGURE. *Pause. A* VOICE *speaks to* THE BOY. *It is
   calm, as though in repose.* THE VOICE *isn't noticeably coming*

from THE FIGURE *or from inside the case; it originates around the case and around* THE BOY. *He shows no surprise at hearing it.*)

VOICE: Why are you staring at me?

BOY: I don't know.

VOICE: What?

BOY: Why I have to look at you.

　(*Slight pause.*)

　What's it like?

VOICE: Very cramped.

BOY (*quickly, shaking his head*): To be dead.

VOICE: I couldn't say.

BOY: Then you're living?

VOICE: No, I'm dead.

BOY: How do you know?

VOICE: How do you know you're alive?

　(THE BOY *pauses.*)

　No one told me anything. No one tells *you*. You just know. . . .

　Before you came, it was very quiet. . . .

　(THE BOY *moves to the end of the case, to study the face.*)

BOY: You don't look dead—

VOICE: I am.

BOY: You look—

VOICE: Like?

BOY: Something else. Like a picture taken of someone sleeping, in the middle of a nightmare.

VOICE (*understanding*): Ahhh . . .

BOY: Why don't you wake up?

VOICE (*definitively*): I'm not sleeping.

　(*Pause.* THE BOY *moves to the other end.*)

　What do you want here?

BOY: I want to know who you are.

VOICE: Now? Nobody.

BOY (*quickly*): I want to know what death is like.

VOICE: Insurance?

BOY: Yeah.

　(*He moves back to the middle of the case.*)

VOICE: I can't tell you that. I can only describe what our life was like.

　(*A slight electric surge is heard, and the spot over the case pulses*

bright and dim once, then returns to normal. THE VOICE
resumes with youthful timbre, but still calm, objective, reflective.)
Morning outside.
Sunrise.
Others sleeping—
   Brothers, sisters—
Deep breath.
Cool air stings my lungs and the smell of last night's cooking is
   heavy on my clothes and blankets.
Rub my hands across my eyes, trying to wake up,
And on my face a beard just starting.
Today will be a good day.
Quietly I lift my spear
To begin the hunt before the others wake.
BOY: What will you hunt?
VOICE: Every morning
   Tracks run by our camp.
   Deep crescent hooves:
   The big deer.
   Caribou.
   If I can bring one back
   It will give us life:
   Meat for muscle
   Skins for warmth
   Bones for our tools
   And fat for cooking grease.
   The big deer is life:
   Food and materials.
      (*Slight hesitation.*)
   We follow the tracks.
BOY: We . . . ?
VOICE: The chill, thick grass
   Crackling underfoot.
      (THE BOY *goes to the left case and turns on the switch that lights*
      up the spear.)
   Sunlight . . .
      (*There is a sound of small bells in the air, which* THE BOY *hears.*)
   . . . Drumming against the leaves of trees:
   Gentle golden bells
   Leading us to the caribou

Deep into the forest.

> (THE BOY *looks forward, intent on seeing the forest and the deer.*
> THE VOICE *also grows more intent, and involved.*)

Hush.
Ahead of us:
A sound
A motion.
We drop
Creep forward.
She stands there
She doesn't see us.

> (THE BOY *very slowly crouches down.*)

She's eating a breakfast
Of grass and berries
Her fur dappled with sunlight:
A ruby-covered cloak.

> (*Slight pause.*)

We will wear her cloak.

BOY (*nodding, rising*): We will wear its—

VOICE: Suddenly!

> (*Accompanied by the loud sound of*)

A twig explodes beneath our feet
Warning her.
She sees us
Standing nakedly
Shies and runs.

BOY: We chase it through the woods!

VOICE: She springs gracefully
  Over dirty pools and thistled shrubs
  That our feet fall heavily upon and tear loudly through.
  She sprints across an open glade
  Lifting and falling as lightly as a sparrow.
  And as we follow
  We crash through the earth
  Suddenly sunk to our knees
  In the moss
  And the rotting leaves.

BOY (*quietly aware*): We're sinking? . . . That's how it happened?

> (*Silence. When* THE VOICE *resumes, it is once more calm,
> objective, in repose.*)

VOICE: We're sinking.

> (*Slight pause.*)

Light comes and goes quickly,
At play behind the clouds
And the sun itself . . .
> Diminishes
Behind the leaves
On the surface
Of the bog.

> (THE BOY *turns off the switch, casting the case with the spear again into darkness.*)

The hunt is done.

BOY (*returning to* THE FIGURE*'s case*): You sank in the swamp?

VOICE: It's warm in the bog, compared to the cold air above.

BOY: You're not in the bog. They dug you up and put you in a case.

VOICE: I'm floating. . . .

BOY: You died very young. Weren't you upset?

VOICE: The deer lived. It flew over the bog. I hear her wings. Beating like a heart. The deer is life. I'm carried on her back. I wear her cloak. I'm sunlight on her fur.

> (*Slight pause.*)

Knowing she's alive, I live. Floating in the bog, I rest. . . . I'm satisfied. The hunt is done.

> (*Brief silence.* THE BOY *walks to the case at right, turns on a switch that illuminates its contents: a deer carcass, seen from behind, and preserved in a similar tanning action as* THE FIGURE *in the center case. The deer carcass has been suspended by two posts, running up under the hip joints, and holding the hindquarters up so the rear hooves are off the floor of the case. This position exposes the stomach and chest, revealing that it's been cleanly gutted: the internal organs are gone. The tanning process has made the carcass a uniform color, however, so there is no contrast between the exterior and interior of the deer, and no suggestion of gore. Its head is not visible. As with the other cases, it is lit with a single overhead spot.* THE BOY *waits.*)

BOY (*forward*): On our way here, we rode the train.

The tracks ran in curves ahead of us.

Everyone said how much wild game we'd see.

But they didn't warn me it would all be dead.

We'd come around a mountainside,

and there'd be another deer that'd walked in front of the train,
    thrown to the cinders at the side of the tracks.
I had a camera with me, and I even bought an extra roll of film.
But seeing all those dead animals,
one dead deer after another,
flying by our window,
legs splayed out in every direction
and their heads rolling on their necks like knotted rags . . .
    (*He stops, shakes his head.*)
I gave up on the idea of taking any pictures.
I'd just track them through the lens. . . .
    (*He goes through the motions, as if holding a camera, making
    clicking noises.*)
And I kept the film in my pocket.
I mean, who wants pictures of a bunch of dead deers?
    (*Slight pause.*)
But one deer really bothered me.
It was hung up on top of a barbed-wire fence by its hind legs.
Looked like it had jumped in the snow and not seen the wire,
and just hung there through the winter 'til the snow began to
    thaw.
With the spring, it had started to decay,
but scavenger birds still opened its belly, so all the life had been
    taken out of it.
Now it was just a dead thing.
A dead thing, hanging there.
Just something to look at.
And I couldn't look away. . . .
    (*He follows it with his head, as though it were passing slowly
    outside his window, while he makes train sounds. He switches off
    the light, and the case and its contents go black.*)
The trip was nearly done.
But as our train pulled into the station,
we passed a little cottage.
And on the lawn, standing upright, surrounded by slush,
was a ceramic deer,
covered with a protective sheet of plastic.
    (*He walks back behind the center case.*)
No sound. No motion.
Just a big ornamental deer, wrapped in a baggie.

(*He stops behind the case, resting his palms flat on its top.*)
And the train stopped, and we got off there—and I knew the
   only way
to really help them was to cover them up in plastic.
   (*Pause.*)
Your deer's gone. It doesn't jump anymore.
VOICE (*slowly*): Why do you say this? You've disturbed my peace.
BOY: Oh, no. You're not sleeping, remember? You're dead, you
   told me.
VOICE (*struggling*): Not deeply dead enough.
   (*Slight pause.*)
What do you want me to do?
BOY: Prove I'm wrong.
VOICE: Ahhh.
BOY: Wake up—Move—Everything's intact. It says so right here.
   There's no reason for you not to be alive.
VOICE (*audibly suffering*): I can't. Breathing's too painful.
   (*A hesitation.* THE BOY *is calm, determined.*)
Why won't you leave me *alone?*
BOY: *I* can't. I need you, to show me you can come back to life.
VOICE (*adamantly*): If I wake up, you'll never rest again.
BOY: I'm not afraid of ghosts—only death.
VOICE: Listen to me—or you'll be sorry: Turn away! Now!
BOY: You're no boogieman, no Freddy Krueger—you're my
   Frankenstein creature. I have to look at you.
VOICE: *I'm warning you*—
BOY: It's already too late.
   (*Pause.* THE FIGURE *suddenly shudders and begins to pull its
   hands in toward its shoulders.* THE BOY *watches, transfixed, from
   behind the display case.* THE FIGURE *pushes itself up from the
   floor of its case, its shoulders trembling with the effort. It reaches
   up one hand, and—to steady itself—pushes that hand forcefully
   against the front glass, with a loud thud. The hand remains
   there, pressed flat against the glass of the case.*)
VOICE: Don't . . . look . . . in my eyes!
   (*A loud crackling or ripping sound is heard, as* THE FIGURE's
   eyelids suddenly open. Its eyes are white. Silence. Blackout.)

The End

Pathological Venus

Brighde Mullins (1964–) was born in Camp LeJeune, North Caro-
lina, and was raised in Las Vegas. Her first play, *The Last Ugly Man in
America,* was produced at the University of Nevada, Las Vegas, in 1983.
Since that time, she has written four one-act plays, four full-length
plays, and an opera. Her plays have been produced at La Mama ETC,
Ensemble Studio Theatre, Yale University Mainstage, George Street
Theatre, the Lyceum in San Diego, and through the Women's Project.
She attended the 1990 Eugene O'Neill Music Theatre Conference for
her opera, *Blue Ceiling,* which was later performed at the University
of Iowa (music by Charles Goldbeck). In 1992 she received a National
Endowment for the Arts Fellowship in Playwriting. Mullins is a 1984
graduate of the University of Nevada, Las Vegas, a 1987 graduate of the
Yale School of Drama, and a 1989 graduate of the University of Iowa
Writers Workshop. She teaches at San Francisco State University in
the graduate creative writing program.

Is there a home where heavy earth
Melts to bright air that breathes
No pain?
—D. G. Rossetti

For the large of limb
the big of bone
and the heavy of heart

Pathological Venus was first produced at the
Yale Cabaret, April 1985. It was directed by
Jennifer McCray, with Patricia Clarkson as
Venus, Patrick Kerr as Kenwigs, and Susan
Knight as Betty Butchko. Music was by
Marcus Giamatti, and the sets were by Philip
Baldwin.

Betty Butchko

Venus

Kenwigs

Man

Woman

Little Boy

Little Girl

Children's Voices

Now

The Betty Butchko Home for Eating Disorders in Sparks, Nevada

(VENUS *is heard singing, breathily, low; the stage is in blackout.*)

VENUS: Let violets gaze upon you

The sunshine's in love with your cheek

What singing bird wouldn't I honor

To say it's her voice when you speak

Snow isn't always in season

And Lent isn't always nearby

But for this deep joy there's a reason

For this dear joy there's a why

So let violets glimmer upon you

The sunshine's in love with your cheek

What singing bird wouldn't I honor

To say it's her voice when you speak

(*Lights up on* BETTY BUTCHKO: *she is a well-groomed middle-ager in florid pinks and spry violets; she wears a veiled pillbox, false eyelashes, heavy rouge. She has a gold-tipped cane; she walks with a slight limp. She speaks into a pink tape recorder and shows slides to the audience.*)

BETTY BUTCHKO: Betty Butchko Home for Eating Disorders, Sparks, Nevada.

(*Shot of a pale pink building.*)

Betty Butchko, founder.

(*Shot of* BETTY BUTCHKO.)

Venus Kenwigs has been mouthing the same words for hours.

(*Shot of* VENUS, *open-mouthed.*)

She's coherent. Moreover, she's fluid. I don't understand the transmogrification she babbles about.

(*Shot of* VENUS *gesticulating.*)

Moreover, she continually contradicts herself.

(*Shot of* VENUS *shaking her head.*)

Her grandfather, Mr. Kenwigs, brought her in on a rope. Dazed, she followed.

(*Shot of* VENUS *with a rope tied around her neck.*)

Delusional hysteria, or a personality disorder. Wounded and dazzled, her hair chopped in harsh angles, betrayed by her body, she says.

(*Return to shot of* VENUS *open-mouthed; fade as lights come up on* VENUS. *She is achingly fat, roped into a slightly raked bed. Her hair is shorn and ruffled. She sings softly as lights come up.*)

VENUS (*there is a breathless joy under her voice; she delights in the rhymes, the rhythms of the lullaby she sings; she is enthused; her face is glowing, beatific; she clutches at the sheets she is swathed in; she sings to the audience)*:

Let violets gaze upon me
The sunshine's in love with my cheek
What singing bird wouldn't be honored
To say it's her voice when I speak.

BETTY BUTCHKO (*shuffling across to* VENUS): Your grandfather brought you to the right place, Venus.

(*Stepping into a harsh, clinical special, twirling her cane.*)

I'll put your ego
Where your id should be

Do a facelift
On your personality

There's another galaxy
For illness and pathology

I'll put your ego where your id should be
Where ego was, id will be
Where ego was, id will be. . . .

(*The special fades;* BETTY BUTCHKO *returns to* VENUS's *bedside, leaning over into* VENUS's *face.*)

BETTY BUTCHKO: Talk into the mike. How long ago were you a child?

VENUS: I was born in Chinquapin. As a baby I spent a lot of time strapped to the kitchen table. I didn't develop depth perception because I wasn't allowed to crawl. There were open pits in the hallway and Mama was afraid I'd fall into one. There was a swamp in our backyard and a Christmas tree in our kitchen. Then my father went to Vietnam, and Mama prayed at the foot of the bed and the crucifix fell off the wall and hit Mama. I was flown to Las Vegas to live with Grandpa.

BETTY BUTCHKO: Do you like living in Las Vegas?

VENUS: City of everyone, and no one has become mine.

At night Las Vegas spreads like spilled diamonds, the last refuge of
the old and immoral, I stay up all night, thinking THIS IS IT, but
no, the sun comes from California every morning, up-a-yellow, westering daisy, ripping my blinds.

BETTY BUTCHKO: Do you have insomnia?

VENUS: What I have is NOT insomnia. It's an infatuation with the
    night.
  You know what I know of the night: It is dark and blue-bright,
  clever cool deep and steep. It waits at my window at twilight and
  dances at dusk on my knees. It pulses, the night, it pulses
  blue-bright, I could nearly get lost in the night. The peculiar
    cool
  of night, like ice cream, it mists up my windows and chills water
  and turns the ivy a shade darker. I lurk through the hallways of
  my grandfather's house, how can anyone sleep among all that
    dark
  beauty, but people do, hip-spinning, moon-grinned, tousled;
    while I
  rearrange flowers, rustle the drapes, turn on the taps, open the
  pantry doors, leaving objects ajar in the night. What is it draws
  me, what is it gnaws me, daring and into the night. I stay
    there, is
  it not all that I need? I will sing night hymn, night is aright then,
  all form and contend in praise for the ways of the night.

BETTY BUTCHKO: We'll call it insomnia.
    (*Beat.*)
  What do you do for a living?

VENUS: I work at the University of Nevada Museum of Natural
    History. I'm a mathematician.

BETTY BUTCHKO: Does this pay well?

VENUS: No one pays you for being quick of wit and mentally
    nimble. So I'm a change girl at the History of Slots Exhibit. I
    change dollars into quarters, quarters into dimes, and dimes into
    nickels.

BETTY BUTCHKO: Isn't this a phony sense of accomplishment, this
    breaking down of dollar bills into pocket change for slots?
    Moreover, all the tourists screaming for nickels—

VENUS: They didn't like my hair this morning.

BETTY BUTCHKO: What happened to your hair?

VENUS: I have roan hair to my shoulders. I live in Chinquapin
    among the
  monarch butterflies, like minor gods, sucking sap in rifts from
  pines. Hordes of monarchs, they alight on my hair, they
    think my

hair is a chestnut tree or a stippled stallion's broad back, I cannot
believe all this riotous color, my hair and the monarchs as dense
as tree sap, insect wonderful, exuberant; me and my mama go to
fish camps after chapel, fish camps with sawdust floors and
buckets of lemon iced tea, it is so hot inside that Mama's
eye shadow melts, so we take our hush puppies to the streamside,
we sit on fallen trees, our necks are prickly-rashed, we are fading
like tea cakes in the sun among the dragon and damsel flies, it's
thick and muggy, and I flip my roan hair to make a breeze
    for me
and Mama, I flip my roan-colored hair, studded with majestic
    and
multicolored monarch butterflies, I flip my hair to make a
breeze.
    (*She shakes and flips her head violently, laughing all the time;*
    her hands go to her hair.)
Bring me a mirror.
    (BETTY BUTCHKO *takes a pocket mirror out of her purse.*)
I have spent a lifetime avoiding mirrors, avoiding plate glass,
avoiding reflective sunglasses.
    (VENUS *runs the mirror over her body contours, never once*
    looking into the mirror.)
But now . . . the chin is firm like granite; the neck, unscathed, a
million kilowatts confirm that there are shoulder blades sharp-
edged and a chest that is serene, a stomach like linoleum,
    thighs of
a child, calves with singularity; it was worth sacrificing the hair.
    (*Singing.*)
Hollow of eye,
Sunken of cheek
Is chic

Narrow of shin
Achingly thin
Is in. . . .

I wear any design, even Italian ones, fringed like a wild thing,
arrivederci Aroma, I could make London broil. What do you
    think
about my cheekbones? I wear my jeans so tight it's hard to get
them over my ankles.

BETTY BUTCHKO: How long have you been this . . . emaciated?

VENUS: Since last night. I prayed for this, I knew it would happen, the gift of prophecy, I didn't work for it, it occurred to me. Things occur. To me. I become enamored with things. I am adaptable, I'm a shape changer, matter is pliable at my touch, physics falters. I was born as Einstein was dying, I profess metempsychosis and psychosis. I am the child born with its father's names in its eyes, my mother claimed to have no fewer than ten brains.

BETTY BUTCHKO: I'm going to have to talk with your grandfather, Venus.

VENUS: I warn you, Grandpapa has never been the same since he got knocked on the head by the chandelier.

> (*Cross-fade to* KENWIGS. *He holds a potato peeler in one hand. He wears a polyester pantsuit. He wears a Caesar's Palace medallion. His hair is slicked back; he throws off strong smells of Old Spice and Skin Bracer because he never washes any of his clothes; he just douses them in cologne. He is slightly cross-eyed and wears thick black corrective glasses.*)

BETTY BUTCHKO (*entering*): Mr. Kenwigs, you brought your granddaughter in this morning.

KENWIGS: They called me at the museum, see. No, see, SHE was at the museum, I was at home peeling spuds, I was thinking of making a stew or a nice hash, see Venus gets a lunch hour nowadays, see—

BETTY BUTCHKO: Mr. Kenwigs, why did they call you from the museum?

KENWIGS: I'm her only alive relative, see—

BETTY BUTCHKO: I'm aware of that—

KENWIGS: See, her daddy was killed overseas, her mama was impaled by a falling crucifix, and I was sent Venus young, see—

BETTY BUTCHKO: I AM AWARE OF THAT. But what happened at the museum?

KENWIGS: Venus pulls this shtick, see, she pretends she's misery-stricken alla time, see, she ain't really—anyway, this morning she walks into the museum happy, beaming, she gots her head wrapped in a floral turban, gots on a miniskirt and white go-go boots, gots a singy-song on her lips, see, and everyone's surprised, see. Cal the security guard calls me, see. Cal says they is not only in awe of Venus's appearance, but Venus is being singy-songy and beaming like a big sunflower. And they is worried. So I put down my spuds and go to see Venus, and there she is, on her steel-reinforced barstool, over and over with the violet lullaby, singing like a banshee. . . .

(*Lights up on* VENUS, *sitting on a barstool in a gentle special, she wears a floral turban of hot pink and turquoise blue on her head, a halter top, a white miniskirt, hot pink tights, and white go-go boots. Her girth is accentuated by the tight, bright clothes. She sings.*)

VENUS: Let violets gaze upon you
The sunshine's in love with your cheek
What singing bird wouldn't I honor
To say it's her voice when you speak. . . .

Hello, Grandpapa.

(*Throws her arms around him, kisses him loudly; he is not used to being treated like this by* VENUS *and is taken aback momentarily.*)

KENWIGS: Venus, you smelled up the whole house. What was you doing last night, creeping around, burning stuff? I found all the windows open, all the cupboard doors open, all the drapes messy. And smoke everywhere.

VENUS: I was praying to Tavia Schultz, who died of acute anorexia nervosa.

KENWIGS: Did you know her?

VENUS: Nope. Got her name out of a medical book. I was praying for a similar affliction, using rituals of the Maori tribe from the Papua New Guinea Exhibit at the museum, and stuff from church on Sunday, Grandpapa.

KENWIGS: Why you calling me Grandpapa?

VENUS: Whyever not?

(*She laughs.*)

A small price for slenderness.

(*She pulls off the flowered turban to reveal her sheared head.*)

KENWIGS: That's what happened. You was burning your hair, huh? That's what I smelled.

VENUS: I was doing rituals started by the Maoris and the Roman Catholics.

KENWIGS: Your hair was your one glory, see. Was gorgeous. Like your mama's. The hair is always the first to go. Your mama died from the top, like a tree.

VENUS: Was your fault for sending her a sharp-pointed crucifix from Tijuana.

KENWIGS: Was nobody's fault. Was God's fault.

VENUS: Don't start on God.

KENWIGS: You don't start on God, by God.

VENUS: Was God that unburdened me.

KENWIGS: I don't know what you think, see. But you is singing and smiling around here like you was Twiggy. And the museum people call me, see, cause they is frankly shocked. And they want me to come get you, see. And plus and added, you is not wearing your museum uniform, Venus.

VENUS: I was not intended by God to wear a muumuu with the state of Nevada embroidered on the back.

KENWIGS: You was not intended by God to wear a miniskirt, Venus.

VENUS: Up until the metamorphosis, I wouldn'ta. But I was transmogrified, Grandpapa.

KENWIGS: They want me to take you away, see, Venus. To talk to people. People who understand this stuff, see.

(*He ties a rope around* VENUS *and leads her offstage. Lights fade as* VENUS *sings the violet lullaby; lights up on* BETTY BUTCHKO *and* KENWIGS.)

So I brought her here, see. She's happy. I never seed her happy since she was twelve years old and was a big kid then, too. She sprouted chins like other adolescents sprouted pimples.

BETTY BUTCHKO: Why was she happy then?

KENWIGS: She wasn't "happy." She cried every night. I called her the dishwasher, she could turn her tear ducts on and off, see.

BETTY BUTCHKO: Why'd she cry every night?

KENWIGS: She cried if someone looked at her the wrong way. But she was happy for twenty minutes once. She sold geraniums in coffee tins to save up for a chandelier she saw at a garage sale. It was old, with lotsa carnival glass and teardrop crystals. It weighed more than she did. She had it hoisted over one shoulder, hunched with her cane, she dragged it home, I watched her from the kitchen window, she lugged it up the driveway and into the hallway and up the stairs and to the den that we turned into her bedroom, and she stood on the lazy Susan and banged it into the

ceiling with butterfly nails. She called me upstairs to look at it, it
filled the whole room, everywhere you stood you were
underneath it, and a dash of sunlight streamlined it all facets and
glintings showered brilliant light in a million prisms of violet and
pink and azure gleams and the chandelier swayed and crystal
brushed cut glass and Venus laughed, her mouth in a red round
O, and at a sudden, at the sound, the chandelier slipped and
pulled half the alabaster ceiling plaster down, and it hit me and
then the linoleum, shards and splinters in my head. Things
haven't been good for me since then, see. But at least I had
things good once. Not like Venus. She just kept getting silenter,
see. She stays up all night eating and watching movies. Then she
goes to work and mopes around the museum all day. That's why
they was so surprised to see her out of uniform and smiling, see.
She seems to have forgotten something enormously complex,
see. Which is why I think you should let her go, see.

BETTY BUTCHKO: I want to do some restructuring, Mr. Kenwigs,
that's all. Some tinkering. What was she like before this
morning?

KENWIGS: Didn't talk much and dressed differently. She only wore
muumuus of purple and green — the colors of a bruise, she said.

BETTY BUTCHKO: Then she was burning up calories
intermittently. . . .

> (*Lights cross-fade to* VENUS; *she wears a purple muumuu with
> the state of Nevada embroidered in outline on the back. She
> wanders in and out of a violet-colored special.*)

VENUS: I walk the cool corridors of my museum,
the stone floor is aching cold, I feel it
through my espadrilles, cold slabs like black
ice floes, I glide among the corridors like a
Rose Bowl float and no one sees me, no eyes that
pry and cut, everything in my museum has been dead
for an hour, a minute, a century. In my museum,
cuttlefish have ten arms and a blunt body,
sauropods are dinosaurs, the dodo is extinct.
The world's largest turtle is seagoing with a
thirty-foot shell, here is a sidenecked tortoise,
a hydromedusa. This is Papua New Guinea, highlands
and lowlands, nose plugs of boar tusks, gold-lip shells
and kingfisher's beaks, a necklace of orchid stems,

headhunting, manhood and religion and a bamboo
man catcher. Here are the polar bears and black
bears, here are lungfish, here are large heart
sea urchins, here is the anatomy of a squid,
here is Costa Rica and Panama, here is the lost
wax method, scarified ware from shallow graves
near the Venezuelan border, offerings of gold,
polychrome and silver, porcelain and emeralds
in a zoned pedestal bowl, next to a fragment
of the Map of the Universe left by Thoth, an
Egyptian god in the guise of a baboon. This
is where offerings are made to a fanged god
whose appetite is voracious and never sated,
warfare is frequent and cruel, the torture
and mutilation of prisoners is a common occurrence,
the marble and plate glass are indifferent,
though, and the dust is fine and as dangerous
as silica, and upstairs, past the katydids
crouched in her fetal bones, there's an
Egyptian woman under Plexiglas, crouched like
a small dog with a bracelet of hounds' teeth and
a skull rotten with decay.

    (*Lights up on* KENWIGS *and* BETTY BUTCHKO.)

BETTY BUTCHKO: The first thing Venus will have to do is quit her
job.

    (*Beat.*)

Working in a place filled with bones is distressing to Venus. She
resents these bones. Moreover, she feels guilty that she's allowed
to go on living while she's surrounded by extinction.

KENWIGS: I don't think so, see . . .

BETTY BUTCHKO: Do you want your granddaughter to go through
life fat?

KENWIGS: I don't care what she goes through life as, as long as she's
happy. She seems to have forgotten her weight. She underwent
something in her sleep—she was up all night, see, cutting and
burning her hair. She's forgotten her size, see.

BETTY BUTCHKO: We'll have to remind her of it.

KENWIGS: Why? She thinks she's thin. She wore a miniskirt to
work. She isn't wearing a tent anymore. For once she's gotten
over herself, see.

BETTY BUTCHKO: Mr. Kenwigs, your granddaughter is hallucinating. She is in a delusional state. She has been committed to an evaluation unit. She could be institutionalized for a very long time. You can either help her rejoin society or you can allow her to wallow in self-induced hypnosis; the consequences are madness and unhappiness; you choose.

KENWIGS: We could prop up a full-length mirror next to her bed and tape her eyelids open; we could make a videotape of her bending over to tie her shoelaces—

BETTY BUTCHKO: Electroshock therapy, and forced reimmersion into her past are recommended treatment. I want to force Venus to relive unpleasant experiences where she was made acutely conscious of her weight.

KENWIGS: There are lots of those, see, Las Vegas isn't a good place to grow up fat. Fat childhoods should be spent someplace else, see; but Venus lost her daddy in Saigon and her mama in Chinquapin, and I'd retired here years ago—I finally said good-bye to the snowdrifts and storm windows of Stamford and the kitchens and pantries of the Roger Smith Hotel and got a multiplex home in Oasis Tropics Retirement Village a Mile Off The Strip. I never planned on turning my paneled den into a bedroom for Venus. I never thought that that crucifix I bought in Tijuana would be so heavy and pointed as to kill poor Venus's mama—I never thought Venus'd get bigger every month on my spud stews and nice hashes—I just know she was a happy eater, see, and I never had enough food as a kid either, and Venus was always healthy, see, her bigness ain't cheeseburgers and hohos, it's spud stews and nice hashes, see—

BETTY BUTCHKO: Girth is girth. Moreover, excess is excess. What was it like for Venus to grow up in a retirement village?

KENWIGS: Well, first of all, it was a violation of the Oasis Tenant Code, see. No children under twelve allowed on the premises, and no one under sixty-five allowed to live in the village.

BETTY BUTCHKO: How old was Venus when she came to live with you?

KENWIGS: Seven. I hadda smuggle her inta the village at three in the A.M. She sat in the corner of the den, never budging, with her knees twisted up over her ears, moaning.

BETTY BUTCHKO: What'd you do to comfort her?

KENWIGS: I fed her. Then she started asking for seconds. Then she started asking for saltines and Seven-Up.

BETTY BUTCHKO: And you gave her whatever she wanted?

KENWIGS: Well, she wasn't demanding, see. She wasn't asking for tap-dancing lessons and Shetland ponies like some kids. Just some more stew, a saltine, a Seven-Up . . .

BETTY BUTCHKO: How long did this go on?

KENWIGS: Coupla months. Then she started moving around, playing; but she hadda be real quiet and not make any little-kid noises or the neighbors would get suspicious.

BETTY BUTCHKO: And she never went out of the house?

KENWIGS: Only at night. She got to sit in the garden. Then Mrs. Shapiro, my neighbor, saw her silhouette and got suspicious. So I dressed Venus up as an old woman and perched her in an armchair and covered her in blankets and introduced her to Mrs. Shapiro as my sister, Rosaleen.

BETTY BUTCHKO: And it worked?

KENWIGS: Majestically. Venus still wears a disguise.

BETTY BUTCHKO: Venus still has to sneak around in a disguise?

KENWIGS: Yeah. But it's second nature to Venus, see. She was always slow-moving and dull-eyed, see.

(BETTY BUTCHKO *takes slight affront.*)

(*Beat.*)

You CANNOT tell me that Venus is sick, though. She's a little confused. And she grew up on healthy foods, like stew with carrots and celery and lotsa Idaho spuds, see.

BETTY BUTCHKO (*shrilly*): I HAVE TOLD YOU THAT EXCESS IS EXCESS.

(BETTY BUTCHKO *steps into a pink special.*)

I was a showgirl for Les Folies Fantastiques. Until I freaked out in a buffet line at the Tropicana Buffeteria and started stuffing potato salad into my bra and getting overwhelmed and singing.

(*She chants.*)

Salami is super
Puts me in a stupor
But, oh, that casserole!

I love the linguini
Spaghets and fettucine
But, oh, that casserole!

The desserts, lime dervish
Are tasty and superbish
But OH that casserole.
   (*She is dreamy-eyed.*)
I love to taste. I do. My hypothalamus is scarred, enough is not
enough. My tongue is smart, my taste buds are geniuses.
   (*In harsh tones.*)
Then I got kicked out of Les Folies Fantastiques. Men stopped
yelling obscenities at me when I walked down the street. Then I
was sideswiped by a Hostess Cupcake truck and spent fifteen
weeks bedridden. Being bedridden and detoxed is the cure for
compulsive behavior. I re-create my salvation for my patients.
After electroshock therapy to simulate being hit by a truck, and
fifteen weeks of detox, my patients begin makeup and exercise
classes.
   (*Stepping out of special.*)
Mr. Kenwigs, how does Venus feel about boys and makeup?
KENWIGS: She never had a date. She used to like makeup, though,
   "MAKEUP IS A SCIENCE," she'd say, "MAKEUP CURES
   NATURE, MAKEUP CURES AN HOUR OF SLEEP AND
   A LIFETIME OF BAD HABITS," she'd say. I'd ask her, "Hey,
   Venus, who are you wearing makeup for?" It's contradictory, see,
   never having a date and slathering on makeup, thick and
   fast. . . .
   (*Cross-fade to* VENUS *in front of a vanity; she wears a terry robe,
   her hair in a towel. She applies makeup, as if before a mirror.*)
VENUS: First of all, MoistureWear foundation, a dab dab dab, then
   smear and watch the creases, ivory beige for a lean look,
   cinnamon dust blush for cheekbones like a Cherokee, then pluck
   stray hairs along the brow line, eyeliner under the lid, blueberry
   eye shadow or sea-opal lilac with silver. Next mascara. Mascara is
   the pièce de résistance, everyone should wear it, babies, old men,
   children. Next, lipstick that doesn't chip, flake or peel in colors
   like Violets Are Fuchsia and Paint the Town Red. Face Powder:
   Cover Girl in a light smattering like Limoges, like porcelain, a
   china doll, although sometimes you WANT to look like a china
   doll.
   (*Surveying her work.*)
Some people should exist from the neck up.
   (*Stretching her arms.*)

Using flesh-colored nail polish makes fingers look longer, slenderer.

(*Beat.*)

You can take away some chins by the strategic use of blusher.

(*Singing.*)

Find me some blond and green-eyed man
Deck him out in Ray Ban shades
Caress his shoulder blades. . . .

(*Beat.*)

What boy would want me? I don't even want me.

(*Singing mournfully.*)

It's little for boys that I care
Statuesque, stunning, or fair
They can keep their deep eyes and their elegant hair
Oh, it's little for boys that I care.

(*Slides up: handsome young men.*)

Although dashing, poetic, and daring
It's not about boys that I'm caring
They can keep their firm chins and their masculine air
Oh, it's little for boys that I care.

(*Slides up: the foods* VENUS *mentions.*)

I'd rather a frosted cannoli
Or a charming chocolate éclair
A plateful of cheese ravioli
A platter of steaks broiled rare
Are decidedly more debonair
So it's little for boys that I care. . . .

> (VENUS *sobs gently, tissuing off the makeup as she sings the last verse; cross-fade to* KENWIGS *and* BETTY BUTCHKO.)

BETTY BUTCHKO (*speaking at first into her tape recorder and then to* KENWIGS): I can re-create this longing by plying Venus with cosmetics after detox. But first we have to force Venus to relive the abject humiliation of obesity.

KENWIGS: How?

BETTY BUTCHKO: Reimmersion in the past. Did people ever make comments that upset her?

KENWIGS: Once we were at a restaurant—Venus didn't like to go out in public much, but it was the anniversary of her coming to live with me—so we was at this restaurant, see—

(*Restaurant sounds: the clinking of cutlery, the low hum of conversation; slides up: a thin couple at a table. The* WOMAN *picks at her salad, the* MAN *stares at his fruit cocktail. They look acerbic. Like they've been sucking lemons. Whenever their voices are heard, there are head shots of them with their mouths open.*)

WOMAN'S VOICE (*loud whisper*): Fat people shouldn't eat in public.

MAN'S VOICE: Or they shouldn't be directly in my line of vision.

WOMAN'S VOICE: She ruins my appetite.

MAN'S VOICE: Look at the excess flesh.

WOMAN'S VOICE: Look at the waste.

MAN'S VOICE: Look at the overdeveloped taste.

WOMAN'S VOICE: But she might not be fat.

MAN'S VOICE: You mean maybe she's preggers?

WOMAN'S VOICE: Maybe, perhaps . . .

MAN'S VOICE: Pregnancy is localized, centralized in the abdomen; this is rampant flesh, fat all over, fat eyes, even . . .

WOMAN'S VOICE: IS SHE FAT OR IS SHE PREGGERS?

  (*Shot of* VENUS.)

VENUS'S VOICE: I ain't pregnant unless it was an immaculate conception. Ask Kenwigs. I never been on a date, despite the makeup and grooming. I was afflicted young.

  (*Beat.*)

Oh that this too, too solid flesh would melt, thaw, and resolve itself on you, then you'd be fat too.

  (*Beat: shot of* VENUS *taking a dainty bite of a burger.*)

One more bite for the poor starving kids in Europe.

  (*Slides fade out as lights cross-fade to* KENWIGS *and* BETTY BUTCHKO.)

BETTY BUTCHKO (*into her mike*): Moreover, Venus can be almost aggressive. . . .

KENWIGS (*interrupting*): She never said anything out loud, see. Or loud enough for anyone to hear. Was always muttering things under her breadth, see.

  (*Beat.*)

Miss Butchko, we should maybe leave Venus alone, see. See how miserable she was? She may be deluded now, dreaming, but at least she ain't moaning and groaning, see.

BETTY BUTCHKO: It's best for Venus to be a coherent and contributing person. This delusional hysteria is fragmentative.

(*Beat.*)
Now, are there any other events that could be re-created to push Venus back into reality?

KENWIGS: There was the time the schoolchildren were mean to her — a whole gang of them stood around her and started singing nasty-like. It took a week for her to recover from that. She wouldn't go out of the house for days, and she won't go near a child.

BETTY BUTCHKO: This was when Venus was very young? What grade was she in?

KENWIGS: This was last month when she was walking past a bus stop.

BETTY BUTCHKO: So the memory is still wet.
(*Beat.*)
Sing, Mr. Kenwigs, SING THAT SONG.
(*Lights up on* VENUS, *humming her violet lullaby.*)

KENWIGS (*singing softly*): I don't want her
You can have her
She's too fat for me. . . .
(*Lights come up brilliantly and swiftly on* VENUS: *she is immersed in purples and greens swirling; she holds her hands over her ears, but the singing gets louder and louder; the singing turns into the voices of children, singing crisply and clearly; then the voices fade as children's voices are heard and their sneering faces come up on slides.*)

LITTLE BOY'S VOICE: Five more pounds and we'll have to declare statehood.
(*There is shrill laughter from the other children.*)

LITTLE GIRL'S VOICE: It's Petunia Pig. Hey, Petunia, how's Porky?

LITTLE BOY'S VOICE: Did you eat him for lunch?

LITTLE GIRL'S VOICE: Fat cow.

VENUS: I was TRANSMOGRIFIED. A divine METAMORPHOSIS. I'm a sylph, a waif, nothing but eyes and hair.

LITTLE GIRL'S VOICE: Blimp.

VENUS: Go away! So I'm fat. So what? Hath not a fat girl thighs? Hath not a fat girl organs, dimensions, senses, affections, passions? Fed with the same food —

CHILDREN'S VOICES: IN LARGER PORTIONS.

VENUS: Hurt with the same weapons —

160 BRIGHDE MULLINS

CHILDREN'S VOICES: IN LARGER SIZES.

VENUS: Subject to the same diseases—

CHILDREN'S VOICES: BIGGER.

VENUS: Healed by the same means—

CHILDREN'S VOICES: FATTER.

VENUS: As a thin person is? If you tickle us, do we not laugh? If you cut us, do we not bleed? If you poison us, do we not die?

> (*The* CHILDREN'S VOICES *have begun singing "I Don't Want Her" again. The voices grow to a pitch; then everything stops altogether; the swirling lights, the* CHILDREN'S VOICES, *and* VENUS *all stop simultaneously;* BETTY BUTCHKO *walks to* VENUS's *bedside.*)

BETTY BUTCHKO (*into her tape recorder*): Moreover, recovery is imminent.

> (*To* VENUS.)

You've surfaced from a nightmare. Congratulations.

VENUS: No. This is the nightmare, this world that was built for speed, not sloth; for the fleet, not the fat. It took me years to forget, and you made me remember. Why?

BETTY BUTCHKO: We want you to rejoin society. Nobody's much use to society when they're hallucinating and confused about their appearance.

> (*She smiles weakly.*)

VENUS (*running her hands over her body slowly*): I hurt again. The end is what I have. And everything hurts me again.

BETTY BUTCHKO: Moreover, we'll start you on the menu plan. . . .

VENUS: There is such a thing as elegance, pity, and hope. Where were you when elegance, pity, and hope were distributed?

BETTY BUTCHKO: You'll eat yellow vegetables and greens for strong bones. . . .

VENUS: My feet live somewhere below me, my bones are a rumor.

> (*Singing gently.*)

I know my sorrow by its way of walking
I know my sorrow by its way of talking
I know my sorrow and it knows me too
And if my sorrow leaves me what will I do
If my sorrow grieves me it grieves my heart too.

BETTY BUTCHKO: You'll lose weight here. . . .

VENUS: I was fine until you came like the dawn and threw fistfuls of ants in my face.

KENWIGS: Miss Butchko wantsa help you, Venus. To help you. That's what you've always wanted, isn't it? Like that time in the underground parking lot, there was a Mustang covered with dirt, and I wrote on the hood WASH ME, and you wrote HELP ME. You're being helped, see. . . . You'll be skinny in a few months, see. . . . You ain't skinny yet, Venus, but time tracks you down, and soon—

VENUS: There is no such thing as soon. My life had been the preparation for VISIONS. I was in a state of BIG DIVINITY, where outsize didn't count. Only insides, a soul like violets, like Easter after Lent and Christmas after Advent. Why did you hafta remind me? I was not made for this dimension.

BETTY BUTCHKO: You'll lose weight . . . moreover . . .

VENUS: No; I am a living monument to pain; I am a flesh sculpture.

BETTY BUTCHKO: Haven't you always wanted to be thin?

VENUS: No; the world isn't good enough. And things are insufficient; and until the world changes with increasing frequency, I will remain fat.

(*Beat.*)

All the time, since I was very young, I've had an incredible emptiness inside of me; I keep trying to fill it up. I ate mustard sandwiches at night to induce visions.

(*Beat.*)

I sleepwalked my days and hogwashed my nights. As I live I weep and as I weep I eat and the hunger and anger and tears get all mixed up to season my food. My food becomes me; this is the secret strategy of being fat. This is what misery is, nothing to have at heart, zero at the bone, a longing to be overwhelmed.

(*Beat.*)

I've reached the point where only death or madness is acceptable.

(*Beat.*)

Dismantle the world; dismantle political systems; dismantle the mechanical regularity of unrequited love and injustice and horror, and I will acquiesce, I will eat your cottage cheese and play racquetball and be like you, Miss Butchko; but first DISMANTLE THE WORLD and BREAK, BLOW, BURN AND MAKE ME NEW.

BETTY BUTCHKO: But everybody wants to be thin—moreover, it's so unhealthy—

VENUS: It's not. I announce my self-loathing to the world, crying
WHAT I DO IS ME, FOR THAT I CAME.
BETTY BUTCHKO: But I've talked to lotsa people like you—
VENUS: And what does the world do with people like me? We watch
you, we yearn for you, we listen to your voices, we admire your
technologies, we swoon over your camaraderies, we die over your
loves, your loves that fall so easily, everything falls easily for you,
we watch you, we remain on the sidelines while your tongues
talk, your technologies succeed, your passionate loves take on
mythological proportions, we are the UNREQUITED of this
world, we sink, we stumble, we fall, we are among you, we are
here today, we are going to stay.
   (*Beat.*)
People like me. I loved the world so much. But no one ever
chose me. You'd think God's heart would break.
   (*Beat.*)
I'm famished. I want fries and a burger.
BETTY BUTCHKO: None of that here. But we have squash and
spinach and deionized water. . . . I thought everyone wanted to
be lean-flanked—I never imagined that fat could be intentional.
   (VENUS *gnaws through the ropes that bind her; she moves her
   bulk slowly out of the bed.*)
KENWIGS: Where are you going?
VENUS: McDonald's.
   (*A mist envelops the stage;* BETTY BUTCHKO *and* KENWIGS
   vanish; slides up of McDonald's; VENUS *ordering;* VENUS *at a
   booth;* VENUS *eating;* VENUS's *voice comes up, singing, as the
   final slides are shown.*)
VENUS: Dig my grave
   Large wide and low
   Place a bowl of tears
   Above below
   Next to a grey-gold mourning dove
   That the world may know
   I died for love. . . .
   (*Lights black out; mist swells as "I'm a Believer" by the Monkees
   plays in a loud burst.*)

The End

CHRISTOPHER DANOWSKI

Family Values

Christopher Danowski (1967–) has lived all but six of his years in the deserts of Arizona. He has also lived in Las Vegas, New York City, and now holes up with his wife, Tamara, in Seattle, where she attends the University of Washington. Danowski finished his schooling at Arizona State University in Tempe, under the guidance of Jim Leonard. He has written over two dozen plays, and at least that many short stories. He has also written two screenplays. His short fiction has appeared in *Hayden's Ferry Review, Journal 500,* and *The Angle.* Six of Danowski's full-length plays have reached full production, including *Rad Art, Running To, Billy's Iguana, Dad's Legs,* and *Drinking without Sitting Down (or Fuck).* Currently, he works full-time in what he terms "a thankless and time-consuming retail machine," but he manages to write during free moments. All told, Danowski says he's happy "but could always use some spare change."

Photo by Tamara Underiner

My mouth is filled with dirt.

—Juan Rulfo, Pedro Paramo

Old Huck
a kid of about twenty, in a ragged black Depeche Mode T-shirt
and brand-spankin'-new black cowboy boots with shiny silver toes

Sharlie
a woman of about thirty, in denim and cotton, barefoot

Alma and Stanislaw
both in their late nineties, dressed in different shadings of old
brown torn cotton

Sonny
a guy of about thirty, in dirty clothes, with a huge X-shaped scar
across his chest

TIME
Right now

PLACE
A twenty-square-foot patch of ground in the hottest part of the
Superstition Mountains; daytime

SET
A simple line drawing on the backdrop to represent mountains and rain clouds. It's monsoon season, so an intermittent
light drizzle happens throughout (can be achieved through sound
alone). Slightly right of center, running upstage to downstage, is
a three-foot-deep wash. A full mesquite tree is up left, and to the
right of this are three tall saguaros, each with two or three arms.

(*Lights up.* OLD HUCK *enters, walks along the center of the wash, carrying a handgun.*)

OLD HUCK: Yup, it's been a long haul for this here Old Huck. It's been like years since fresh water, air-conditioning, and maybe an iced tea with lemon and sugar. Oh, yeah. But they're not bringing this Old Huck down. Not a chance. Let me tell you what. My dad won't let me have the truck—fuck him. He won't understand. This is what it's like. This is me here now. This is me talking. Kicking over rocks. Doing whatsoever I may please. Oh, yeah. Think I'll smoke me a clove.

(*He lights a clove cigarette and steps out of the wash, smoking and meandering.*)

Mm. Like a baked ham in your lungs. This is living. Think I'll shoot me a cactus.

(*He fires a shot and misses. Looks around. Beat. There's no one around to have seen him miss.*)

This is living. Think I'll shoot me a cactus.

(*He fires a shot and knocks a big chunk out of the trunk of a saguaro. Long pause. He grins wildly. Starts shooting it to pieces.*)

Yeah, that's right, Dad! One day, that's right, one day, I'm gonna buy me my own truck. Oh, yeah. Run you right over. Oh, yeah. That's me. That's me talking. That's what I'm gonna do.

(*He walks right up to the cactus and aims up at an arm.*)

Yeah, sure, I'll go get the groceries, I'll take out the trash, I'll get you a spumoni from up the block. Yeah, sure I will. And while we're at it . . . fuck you, Dad!

(*He fires the gun and hits the arm. It falls off the cactus and onto* OLD HUCK, *killing him. Silence for a few beats. We hear footsteps and singing from far off. As it gets closer, we make out the words to Bob Dylan's "Isis."* SHARLIE *enters, walks through the area. She does not see* OLD HUCK. *She stops in the center of the wash. She lays a single flower on the ground and keeps walking and singing.*)

SHARLIE: "I still can remember the way that you smiled,
On the fifth day of May in the drizzling rain."

(*Exits.*)

(*Long silence. We hear soft giggling. The giggling continues, and the source—* ALMA *and* STAN— *emerges from behind the mesquite tree. They walk over to the cactus and survey the damage.* STAN *kicks at the cactus a little.* ALMA *picks up the gun, sniffs it, and throws it offstage.*)

ALMA: Now there's a bad sign.

STAN: We've seen worse. It's not the end of the world, Alma.

ALMA: Stanislaw, I wouldn't be so smug if I were you.

STAN: Right, right.

(*They giggle some more, walk to the wash, and sit on opposite banks. They talk to the ground between them, where the flower lies.*)

ALMA: When we were just nine years old, we learned how to sleep through storms.

STAN: We were ten, Alma. She always gets this part wrong.

ALMA: We were nine.

STAN: No, no. Definitely ten.

ALMA: Well, say we were both nine years old. And on the day before our tenth birthday, we learned how to sleep through the storms.

STAN: This is my favorite part.

ALMA: We took an old cardboard box . . . Was this when we still lived in the house?

STAN: I don't remember.

ALMA: It was a real nice house, too, Sonny. You would have seen it and said, "That's real nice. That house there. It's a real nice house."

STAN: It was a real nice house, Sonny.

ALMA: And we'd take turns between sleeping in the box and standing guard.

STAN: With a big pile of rocks.

ALMA: That's right. With a big pile of rocks. And that's when I learned how to throw so well.

STAN: But only at people. That was the important thing. We were very careful to only hit people.

ALMA: That's right. And that's when I learned how to hit people, usually in the head, and Stanislaw learned how to miss them. To throw just close enough to scare them off.

STAN: I always missed on purpose.

ALMA: That's what he always says. And so we'd get through the storms.

STAN: It was on purpose. Tell him it was on purpose.

ALMA: He heard you.

STAN: Make sure he knows that. It's important.

ALMA: Okay, okay. Sonny . . . Stan always missed on purpose, or so he said. It became his skill. His one real skill. And he eventually got so good that he could even aim at the broadside of a barn and not hit it. And this skill became so widely known that people would come from miles around just to have rocks thrown at them.

STAN: Stop.

ALMA: And, oh, how they loved it. They would come to see these famous rocks fly past their heads, and, oh, how they would laugh.

STAN: That's enough.

ALMA: And after they were done laughing at how Stanislaw would pretend to miss, he would then pretend to cry. And I don't mind telling you about how that brought the house down.

STAN: I've had it.

>*(He throws a rock at her. It misses, but it's enough to bring her out of her story. She stares at him. Long beat. He throws three more rocks at her in succession. They all miss. She hurls a rock back, and it hits him square in the head.)*

Ow! Ow! Ow!

>*(Holds his head and runs in circles.)*

ALMA: Stan! Stan! I'm sorry, Stan!

>*(Crosses the wash to him.)*

Stan!

STAN: Ow! Ow! Ow!

>*(He holds his head and runs in circles.)*

ALMA: Stan!

STAN: Ow! I'm bleeding! Ow! I'm bleeding!

>*(Runs in circles.)*

Ow! I'm dizzy!

>*(He passes out.)*

>*(Long pause. She stares at him. Beat. She crosses back to the wash and sits on the bank, talking to the flower.)*

ALMA: Sonny, I am very worried these days. Something in the air— I'm not trusting it for a second, this something. I don't trust it. Sonny, if there is only one thing I want you to know, it's that it has not always been this way. Now, Sonny, it has always been hard. That's not how I mean. Not that it's getting harder. It's not. But something has shifted. Something very important has been moved from its place. Now. If I were your mother, Sonny, I would tell you to sleep for a hundred years. That is what I would do. But I can't do that. I'm not your mother, Sonny, and I am just too worried these days to comfort you like a mother would. In fact, I want you to wake up, and so I am going to make you some coffee.

> (*She digs up some coffee beans and puts them in a grinder she keeps in a bag around her waist. She puts all this in a cup, also from her bag. She sets this on the bank of the wash. She pulls* STAN *off with her, back behind the mesquite tree. Long pause. The ground beneath the flower begins to move and shudder, until it breaks open, and* SONNY *comes up. He is covered with dirt.*)

SONNY: Oh, boy. What I wouldn't give for a nice hot cup of joe. Hey.

> (*Sees the coffee and pulls himself up to the bank. Sits and sips.*)

SHARLIE (*enters with a shovel*): Aw, you're already up.

SONNY: That's right, Sharlie, and I'm awfully sleepy-eyed. Don't even talk to me until I get a cup of coffee in me.

SHARLIE: I was gonna undig you.

SONNY: Don't even talk.

SHARLIE: You're so lucky. I didn't even get a coffee today yet. I didn't even have time, I've been so busy. I'm running around, trying to get my list of errands done, and you're already up, and you got this coffee. That's just so lucky. You're so lucky.

SONNY: As if this came outta thin air. As if it were that easy. That's funny.

> (*Calls to tree.*)

Hey, Alma, Sharlie here thinks this came outta thin air. Is that funny?

ALMA (*from behind tree*): That's funny, Sonny.

SHARLIE: As if I didn't know. I know where coffee comes from, Sonny. I'm just amazed at it. I'm just looking at you with that coffee, amazed.

> (*Beat.*)

SONNY: That's all?

SHARLIE: That's it.

SONNY: Well, come on over here, then, and we'll both be amazed at it at the same time.

SHARLIE: Like in sharing?

SONNY: Something like that.

SHARLIE: Like in half?

SONNY: Yeah, or in a close approximation of a half.

SHARLIE: That's only half-awake.

SONNY: Yeah, but your half-awake and my half-awake makes a whole person awake all together.

SHARLIE: Oh, that's romantic.

SONNY: Yeah, I'm always coming up with stuff like that.

(*They sip the coffee together for a few beats.*)

Now I'm feeling a lot better. Like in a contemplation state. Where I can just sit here and contemplate. As if being awake and out isn't a bad thing at all. I can just sit here, and sip this coffee here, and look at this dirt here, and feel this rain coming down here, and just see all this, and there's nothing to worry about in it. There is no danger here. This is just great here.

SHARLIE (*points*): Rattlesnake.

SONNY: Where?

(*Starts to get up.*)

SHARLIE: I'm kidding.

(*Pause.*)

So what are your feelings on that dead guy back there?

SONNY (*looks; shrugs*): He looks pretty dead.

SHARLIE: You're just gonna let him lie there?

SONNY: Uh-huh. Do him some good to lie there a while. Take in the desert air. Builds character.

SHARLIE: I don't know, Sonny. Now I'm just a worldly city girl by nature, but where I come from, we bury our dead.

ALMA (*from behind the tree*): Pay attention, Sonny, this is important.

SONNY: I'm not giving up my bed. Look at it, it's finally all soft, the way I want it. And with a real pretty flower next to it, to boot. No. I'm not giving that up. Not today. I like waking up there. I feel light. Good dream. It's a comfort. This whole place is a comfort to me. You should try getting closer into the ground, Sharlie. Help you remember.

SHARLIE: So that's that.

SONNY: For now.

SHARLIE: For now.

(*Beat.*)

I don't want to alarm you or anything. But there's only a few hours of daylight left. And then the moon comes out. Hm. Well, there's moonlight, too. Hm. I suppose there isn't anything to get alarmed about after all.

SONNY: You almost put a scare in me.

(*Calls to tree.*)

Hey, Stan, she almost put a scare in me.

STAN (*behind tree*): Just stand your ground, Sonny. This is your home. Remember that. No one can hurt you at home.

(*Beat.*)

Ow! My head!

ALMA (*behind tree*): I'm sorry, Stanislaw.

STAN (*behind tree*): Good shot, though.

ALMA (*behind tree*): Thanks, Stan.

(*Beat. As* SHARLIE *speaks,* SONNY *digs a small hole, puts her feet in the hole, and covers them with dirt.*)

SHARLIE (*staring at the tree*): It's amazing. This is really amazing. How they erupt like that. And then everything's calm again. So that's how it is here. I could get used to it. It's not like one wave of calm after another. I don't think I could even imagine living like that for very long. Where I come from, it's like a constant, sudden cloudburst. Like thunderbolts are always crashing around everywhere. It's okay. It's really not bad. You just have to duck a lot. You get used to it. It's like that in lots of places. I've been lots of places, and it's like that. You get used to it. But now when I come here, every day, part of me remembers. I mean wonders. Part of me wonders about here. As in what's so bad about here. But then part of me begins to forget. I mean, begins to long. Part of me begins to long for all those things I used to have, and I begin to miss those things. Like the smell of diesel. Tastee-Freez ice cream. Or a really neat, colorful box with a hamburger in it. The kind of comfort that you just can't grow. These are the things that can really free you. They really can. They make you lighter. You get them, and you have them, and that's it. Then you can float for a long time. Then, if you should land, you can do it again. And it just gets better each time. And you get lighter each time. To the point where it feels like this is what you were born to do. Like this is the place you were born out of. This concrete, this pavement, the grease, the metal, the smoke is your real home. And there's no reason to leave. It's what makes you light.

(*Long pause.*)

SONNY (*calls to tree*): Hey, Alma, Stan! Looky! I just grew me a girl!

ALMA (*behind tree*): Nice handiwork, Sonny!

STAN (*behind tree*): Hoo-ey! A big 'un, too!

ALMA (*behind tree*): In these rains, bet she'll grow twice her size if you take good care!

> (*This freaks* SHARLIE *out, and she tries to get her feet out. Eventually, she passes out from the effort, feet still in the ground.*)

SONNY: I've been trying to catch you for a long time. You always came, but you never stayed. Now I have you. Now I got you. I feel light now. You're right, Sharlie. You want stuff, then you get stuff, and you feel light. I feel light.

> (*Crosses to her, sits next to her, and kisses her.*)

And so, now that I'm awake, I'm just left wondering. We could build us a nice bed. Or maybe a big house to put the bed in. With central air-conditioning and a combination refrigerator to keep ice and water in. We could do that right here. We could build it right here. We could run away from this place and never come back. We could raise rabbits, or make jewelry, or get a car. We could buy a couple ties and go to work. We could do lotsa things.

> (*Beat. He stares at her for a long time. He digs a hole next to her, sticks his feet in the hole, and covers it over. He stares at her. He kisses her neck, puts his arm around her, and sleeps. Long beat.* ALMA *and* STAN *come out from behind the tree,* STAN *with a white bandage on his head. They roll the body of* OLD HUCK *into the wash and cover him over with dirt. Over this they lay the flower. They sit on the same side of the bank, facing away from* SONNY *and* SHARLIE. *They stare at each other. The sound of rain gets louder.*)

STAN: It's picking up.

ALMA: Uh-huh. Never used to rain this hard.

STAN: That's right.

ALMA: Not this time of year.

STAN: That's right.

ALMA: I'm not sure what it means. I'm not sure if I trust it.

STAN: It wasn't always this way.

ALMA: That's right.

STAN: Maybe we shoulda had kids.

ALMA: We can always adopt.

STAN: That's true.

ALMA: I bet we'd be good at it. We could take them under our wing. Teach them what we learned here. We could have long, full days together here. Get to know the ground, the wind, the rain, the lightning. All of it. Get to know it all together. Just you and me and the kids. And everything else around here. We could throw rocks at each other. We could make coffee for each other. We could bury each other. We could sleep next to each other. Get rained on with each other. For years and years it would go on like this. And then, on some hot, rainy day, when we're in our twilight years, you and I could sit together and reflect. We'd look back on everything we did.

STAN: On everything we found.

ALMA: On everything we lost.

STAN: And we'd watch the rains come.

ALMA: And cover the ground with water.

STAN: And begin to overflow.

ALMA: And turn into a river.

STAN: With a current so strong it was as if it came from the sky itself.

ALMA: And we sit by the riverbank.

STAN: As the sun goes down.

ALMA: As the river begins to fill.

STAN: And overflow.

ALMA: And the desert becomes the ocean again.

STAN: And the desert becomes the ocean again.

ALMA: And washes this all away.

STAN: And washes this all away.

> (*The rain gets louder. They stare at the flower.* SHARLIE *and* SONNY, *eyes still closed, feet still in the ground, slowly begin to rise, slowly extending to their full height, and, as if in a dream, just when it seems as if they've stretched themselves as high as they possibly can, they stretch higher. And the lights dim.*)

The End

Zombie Chick

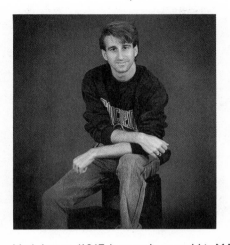

Mark Jensen (1967–) recently earned his M.F.A. in playwriting at the University of Nevada, Las Vegas. Originally from Minnesota, he has had plays produced in California, Minnesota, Nevada, and Virginia. The University of Nevada, Las Vegas, has performed several of his plays, including *Burning Tar, Garden of the Mind, Rocks, The Conceited Terrorist,* and *Hoghouse.* Jensen also collaborated with University of Nevada, Las Vegas's Senior Adult Theatre Program to create an oral history piece entitled *Seasons,* which was later presented at the 1993 National Council on Aging Convention in Anaheim, California. Brainerd Community College of Minnesota staged *Weldings* for Jensen in 1992. The University of Virginia, Charlottesville, premiered his *Pre-Matrimonial Conversation.* Most recently, City Lights Theatre Company of San Jose premiered two of his one-acts, *Hoghouse* and *Grave,* as their first production of Late Nights at City Lights. Mark is a member of the Playwrights' Center of San Francisco. He lives in San Jose, California.

Zombie Chick received a reading at the Playwrights' Center of San Francisco on January 7, 1994.

CHARACTERS

Sue
a teenage girl who can raise small animals from the dead

Mooncloud
*a woman in her late twenties; a member of a Wicca Coven in
Las Vegas*

TIME
Present day

PLACE
A remote ranch in the Southwest. It is a hot afternoon.

(SUE, *a plain teenage girl in jeans and a T-shirt, sits on a tractor tire sewing on some coveralls. A large cardboard box sits next to her. She hums. One crudely painted sign sits a ways off. It says See the Chicken Five Bucks. Another sign above* SUE *says Chicken Here. Enter* MOONCLOUD, *dressed in black clothing and carrying a large bag. She wears power crystals and other talismans.*)

MOONCLOUD: Where's the chicken?

SUE: Five bucks.

MOONCLOUD: Right, right. This better be real. I flew all the way out from Vegas. The airplane food was terrible, some sort of hard bun and a stale salad. Almost as hot out here too. You ever been to Vegas?

(MOONCLOUD *hands* SUE *a five-dollar bill.* SUE *says nothing but takes the lid off the cardboard box.*)

Doesn't sound like it. So this ranch is where the spirits called me. The girls are probably having a huge laugh fest back at the coven. I'm sure this is right, though. I'm sure this is right and you're the one.

SUE: Heat affecting your marbles?

MOONCLOUD: Bring the chicken out. I paid my five dollars!

SUE: Good thing Ruth could use another stroll.

(*They are quiet.*)

MOONCLOUD: A long flight, it's what it is today. Sorry.

SUE: Come on now, chick, chick, chick! That's right, baby, c'mon. Here she is.

(SUE *takes a baby chick out of the box. There are pink ribbons around its neck, which* SUE *uses as a leash.*)

This is Ruth, the Amazing Zombie Chicken. Ruth, this is . . . somebody else.

MOONCLOUD: It is alive!

SUE: Once you've seen enough, she's back in that box. I'm not sure this sunlight's too good for her feathers.

MOONCLOUD: I wasn't expecting it to be so . . . The head was chopped all the way off?

SUE: Sure was.

MOONCLOUD: So what happened? What did you do?

SUE: You want the short version or the whole story?

MOONCLOUD: The whole version.

SUE: All right. Another dollar.

MOONCLOUD: Here. Now okay! What did you do?

SUE (*she tells this a hundred times a day*): Dad was working on the hay mower, and the little twerp got his head up in the sickle. Dad rolled the chain and clip. I started bawling so hard. I saw it right from this tire. Some kind've rumbling grabbed at my intestines. Had to go over to it, must've been a supernatural something or other.

MOONCLOUD: Describe it some more. We'll see.

SUE: What you sayin'? Ruth's chirping, ain't she?

MOONCLOUD: I'm a pagan, honey. I've had a little experience with these things. So go on, go on! Go on.

SUE: Jeeze. I grabbed my needle and thread and marched up to the sickle. Snatched up her head and the body, and I just started sewing. Clouds were worked up swirling around me, and the ground was shaking so hard the barn almost collapsed. Could hear the two-by-fours cracking in the walls, and I still tell Dad he should get a carpenter to check out the building. But the old skinflint don't wanna part with the money. Never listens anyways. Well, I sewed that last stitch on the neck there—you see it there? Take a look, there's a stitch on his neck. I ain't saying a thing more until you notice it, 'cause I sure ain't lying.

MOONCLOUD: Yes, yes there is a big stitch!

SUE: Whole body turned reddish orange and then blue, then black. All this moaning was going on, and then this mist popped up and floated away. So there she was, scratchin' and chirpin'. Named her Ruth right on the spot.

MOONCLOUD: Wow.

SUE: Yup.

MOONCLOUD: It is you. You have the gift.

SUE: Folks say I got something. Don't know what it is, really.

MOONCLOUD: You're coming back with me to Vegas. Here's my card. Our card. I'm Mooncloud, I'm from the Druidic Council. We need a prophet like you to save our coven. You're the one.

SUE: Ma'am, you're getting wild.

MOONCLOUD: There's been visions. A girl and her chicken, every night when we burned candles!

SUE: Oh, great. Dad! Dad!

MOONCLOUD: Hear this out, Honey!

SUE: You're seeing Ruth, and that's as far as things go here.

MOONCLOUD: We're your religion come true! You're a voodoo sorceress!

SUE: Hell, no, I'm a Presbyterian!

MOONCLOUD: You made the chick live, you're the prophet! Okay, okay, before you say no completely, just let me describe the complete package.

SUE: I'm taking down the whole business. Bringing all sorts here. Too many sorts for me.

(SUE *starts taking down her signs.*)

MOONCLOUD: We're your kin, Sister. In some ways. I'm a follower of the Earth, the Sun. We've got a huge coven up in Vegas. In fact, we meet every week in a strip mall close to downtown. Now, please, please hear this through. There's no hope at all without you! There's been terrible luck last week.

SUE: You've seen the chick. I got patches to finish.

MOONCLOUD: The owners are planning on evicting us, and we can't find another place to meet. No one will rent to Wiccans. But see, if you came, and if you convince the sisters, we'll make you Head Enchantress. Think of that! Tourists will come from all over the world, bringing their dead pets. You could sew them up. Your thunder and lightning would happen. Then pow! Your miracle, the pet reborn. Tourists will convert, pay homage to our true temple. You'd create a holy city. All because of this gift.

SUE: It ain't nothing special. Just something that happened.

MOONCLOUD: We've got a ticket for you.

(MOONCLOUD *digs in her bag and takes out an airline ticket.*)
Our coven's waiting for your direction.

SUE: My what? Direction, you said? No way. Dad!

MOONCLOUD: Why call him, huh? Don't run off! Sue, Sue, let's sit by the tire. All right, easy, easy. We won't talk about Vegas anymore. I've got you spooked with this wild talk, I can imagine. A free plane ticket doesn't come every day. Come on, Sue, settle back down. Here, do your sewing. Please. I'll just sit with you. Won't say a word, we'll sit and . . . and we'll sit.

SUE: I won't sit.

MOONCLOUD: Okay. But I don't want your papa in on this. I know what fathers say. Just . . . You sew really well. This is pretty.

SUE: Something I've always been able to do.

MOONCLOUD: Not me. I'm terrible.

SUE: Yeah.

MOONCLOUD: I am really terrible.

SUE: That don't matter. It just takes a little practice.

MOONCLOUD: It would take more than practice for me.

SUE: I ain't sitting by you.

MOONCLOUD: Hey, I can't blame you for that. A woman declares
she's a pagan, right on your own farm. I'd flip out too if someone
came and said that. But I can't even sew.

(MOONCLOUD *holds out* SUE's *patchwork.* SUE *takes it.*)

SUE: I was pretty much plain-Jane 'til I sewed on the chick's head.
Enjoyed the changes first, figured I'd like people noticing me.
That's gotten real old.

MOONCLOUD: Forgive my excitement. I must've bothered you in a
big way. I just could not believe my visions turned out real.

SUE: It's just like when I puked at church, and fat ladies were
gawking at me and giving me Rolaids. Couldn't stand that!

MOONCLOUD: People bother you a lot?

SUE: Don't got much time for 'em. They bring dead kids. I can't
stitch them up. It only works on the pets. I keep telling people
that, but pretty soon down the road comes another baby in a
casket.

MOONCLOUD: You're seen as a savior.

SUE: I don't want that!

MOONCLOUD: The spirits chose you. There's no denying what
they've made you into.

SUE: There should be.

MOONCLOUD: The Earth spirits taint their blessings. It's part of
their way.

SUE: Earth spirits.

MOONCLOUD: They gave you the talent.

SUE: Whatever. It sucks.

MOONCLOUD: Just come to Vegas and heal the pets.

SUE: I think that's your five dollars' worth.

MOONCLOUD: Do you like being here?

SUE: I've always been. Don't know anything different.

MOONCLOUD: Yes, you do.

SUE: I don't know anything different.

MOONCLOUD: They friendly? People here? Oh, sure, they notice
you. They notice you like they watch a two-headed goat.

SUE: Yeah.

MOONCLOUD: You'd be one of the sisters.

SUE: But it's . . . leaving.

MOONCLOUD: Doubt it'd be much of a loss.

SUE: Is the sky this color?

MOONCLOUD: Everything you got now you'd get again. Plus the sisterhood.

SUE: But is the sky this color?

MOONCLOUD: Sue's no name for a sorceress. Something like Lavinia Magica, that's more the thing. Now that's a name that would draw in Vegas.

(SUE *laughs*.)

MOONCLOUD: What?

SUE: Lavinia Magica?

MOONCLOUD: Came off the top of my head. The coven will dream up a better name, but see, see your possibilities? And this is all because you got the power in you. Use it! The power, the talent. It can't dry out on this tire. Think of the pets you could heal! Five dollars a pop, that's nothing!

(MOONCLOUD *grabs the See the Chicken Five Bucks sign and rips it up*.)

Try getting five times five times five hundred dollars!

(*They are quiet*.)

Well, maybe it only seems exciting to me.

(SUE *shrugs her shoulders*.)

Let's put Ruth back in her box.

SUE: Sure.

(MOONCLOUD *picks up* RUTH *and puts her away*.)

Don't let other folks pick her up normally. Think she's still healing.

MOONCLOUD: Oh, I'm sure it will take time. But she's so healthy. It's spreading to me. You could save people through their pets.

SUE: The people would haveta stay out. Wouldn't wanna be associating with people at all. Keep 'em outside by those neon lights or whatever. Just wanna see their dead animals.

MOONCLOUD: That is a yes.

SUE: Oh, no, I was thinking maybe, but—

MOONCLOUD: I'm sure I heard a yes in there someplace. Don't back off now. No way you can.

SUE: It's too far!

MOONCLOUD: Shake and we'll bake!

>   (MOONCLOUD *shakes* SUE's *hand.*)

We'll turn that strip mall into a temple! Let's celebrate what's happened. Prove good faith, Sue, let's make a covenant between each other!

>   (MOONCLOUD *takes out a wrapped-up bundle.*)

My hamster. Got squished in the door.

SUE: Oh, no.

MOONCLOUD: Came home late after a meditation. I was all messed up. It was just announced the coven was closing. Slammed the door wide open. Heard his little shriek . . .

>   (SUE *strokes the hamster, then stops.*)

SUE: Thought you believed me.

MOONCLOUD: Oh, I do, ya'know, I do. I do. But the sisters aren't swayed.

SUE: You said you believed me. Now I gotta give a performance?

MOONCLOUD: Heal the hamster for the coven. It's for a plane ticket. The girls all chipped in for the flight. You need to prove to them you are who you are.

SUE: There are tons of satisfied pet owners. You could call 'em!

MOONCLOUD: You got problems with people, so do we. The coven doesn't trust anyone. We lost our lease without a notice, without a reason! It was gone. All the money left to us is in these two tickets. I believe, Sue, I believe. And if I can bring back a living hamster, then I can bring back you.

SUE: When I told you about Ruth, I, ah, I was spinning some color on the story. I mean, the lightning and the earth quaking. Those parts ain't particularly real. You'll see it's not flashy.

MOONCLOUD: Honey. Resurrect the pets. We'll make the lightning.

>   (SUE *picks up her needle and thread.*)

What kind of preparation do you need?

SUE: None. It's all in the sewing.

>   (SUE *starts. There's a small howl from the hamster.*)

This one's gonna get pretty crazy sounding.

MOONCLOUD: Each stitch is driving off death. I'd howl too.

SUE: There's smoke when it's almost over.

MOONCLOUD: Make our hamster live, Sue, make it live.

SUE: There. One more stitch.

>   (*Smoke. When the smoke is gone,* SUE *is seen holding a live hamster. They watch it move.*)

MOONCLOUD: A new religion is born. You're a prophet, Sue. A modern prophet.

SUE: Getting better at it, seems like.

MOONCLOUD: One plane ticket for Lavinia Magica, Raiser of the Dead!

(MOONCLOUD *gives* SUE *the ticket.* SUE *takes it.*)

SUE: What's the climate gonna be like out there, anyway?

The End

WESTERN LITERATURE SERIES